Oh My God

The Way Is Within

SHER GILL Galib

Grosvenor House
Publishing Limited

The right of Sher Gill to be identified as the author of this
work has been asserted in accordance with Section 78
of the Copyright, Designs and Patents Act 1988

The book cover is copyright to Sher Gill
Cover image to iStock image by mycola - sunset over sea

This book is published by
Grosvenor House Publishing Ltd
Link House
140 The Broadway, Tolworth, Surrey, KT6 7HT.
www.grosvenorhousepublishing.co.uk

A CIP record for this book
is available from the British Library

Paperback ISBN 978-1-80381-185-7
Hardback ISBN 978-1-80381-186-4
eBook ISBN 978-1-80381-187-1

First published: 23-11-2018

Website: www.shergill.uk.com
Email: beingasaint@gmail.com

SHER GILL Galib

CONTENTS

INTRODUCTION

'Where is God? It is everywhere in the state of consciousness within each soul for us to experience and feel its presence. I have expressed in my writings that every person can make the journey within and God is waiting for you. God has infinite qualities and is beyond our knowing but if you manage to experience one glimpse of God in your life, you can consider yourself lucky and your journey has been worthwhile. I have had the privilege to be in the presence of God since I was a child.

I have seen and lived in the presence of God beyond anyone's expectations or knowing. When I was in the presence of God in march 2008, I was told to express its presence in 250 chapters. God is like a holy tree that has so many branches and each chapter is an individual branch of this holy tree and expresses God's knowledge or its qualities for us to experience. It was a huge task and I asked this question within; 'How is it possible for me to write 250 qualities of God?

To write about one quality of God is difficult and I am not a professional writer. An answer came; All you have to do is hold a pen in your hand and Spirit will do the writing. That was a significant relief. This is the fifth book and I have managed to write two hundred and fifty branches of this holy tree. There are over forty chapters in this book and each expresses God-knowledge and answers many questions.

The first chapter is called God; 'Who Am I? It is based on how man-made religions mislead the followers and fail to express how to experience God's presence in this lifetime. Religions today don't believe in having a living Master. This is why they fail to understand the factual content of its spiritual writings. The living Master can explain the actual contents of any spiritual writing and guide the Seeker to go within in the presence of God. The living Master does not rely on any spiritual works written by someone else.

God has invested more than enough spiritual knowledge within this individual; he can write his holy books. I remember asking this question to Spirit many years ago, knowing that I didn't have any holy book which I could claim as my own. The answer came; You will write your own. When the flow of Spirit comes, I hold the pen in my hand and Spirit does the writing. Each chapter leads the Seeker closer to God. May you enjoy reading and making your life worthwhile. The present moment is the kingmaker.

It Just is. Every is-ness is like a drop of rain that disappears into the sand without a trace while you are watching. So, make the most of your present life because each moment will lead you in the presence of God if used wisely.

GOD; 'WHO AM I?

I am the way and the way is within. To reach me is so simple. Once you decide, sit down and chant, 'Haiome,' which means, 'I will meet you.' It also means, 'I am here to meet you; soul knows its way home.' In Anami, we were one, you are far since Religions came in. I will be here, waiting for you like a good father waiting for his lost son. Listen to the voice within, the vehicle is sound and the light will show the way.

When you are here, you will know, feel and ask within, 'Have I been away or was it just a dream? The lower worlds were only foreign land and it was only an experience. But those souls who are still on the physical plane think I am far away. You know I am as close as your heartbeat. One day, all will know I am here. 'Are you in the kingdom of bliss? Since religions came, man's direction of search has changed. I am waiting for them and they are worshipping idols.

Then a question arises, 'Who am I? All religions agree there is only one God. I am the creator of all creation but no one approaches me. You have created the riddle but I show you the way is within. You may fail to reach me but many have succeeded and so can you. I am not beyond knowing or unreachable. Follow my spiritual man on earth, he will never fail you. The riddle is this, I exist beyond time and space, therefore, it is difficult to see me. But at the same time, I have given you the capability of travelling beyond time and space to visit me.

Your mind does not let you go because it is the lover of illusion, which is temporary and it is created for a purpose. What is seen visually is an illusion and what is unseen is eternal. A pilgrimage is not to the temples for my search. It is the journey within, where I am waiting for all my creation. I have created the riddle to amuse the minds. It is similar to a maze, you go in circles and come back to the same point because all the paths seem the same.

I am so close yet so far at times. All spiritual planes are far, yet they are within each soul and are within your reach. The day you solve this riddle, I will be close to your heart and you will say, 'I know, God.' You travel thousands of miles to look for me in the temples. 'Do you think you will find me there? No, I do not live there or am trapped within four walls. I am everywhere. Those who try to erase my name are those who have turned their backs on me.

They are looking for me but in the wrong places. I am residing within each soul, this is why you cannot see me. Try to feel my presence as you walk along and feel uplifted spiritually. The time will come when you will know me more. All religions are living in history and mythology. I do not live or breathe in history or mythology. I am present if you want to feel my presence. No religious person will come near me until you come to universal thought via reciting holy verses and acting on them.

All religious people are too busy with their chores, family problems and praying, not to me but some pictures of gurus or statues. This is why I do not answer their prayers. I want to listen to their cries but they do not want me to hear. They are expecting the statues to attend and I wish they could. This world is full of stones and some are praying to trees and tying some colourful strings to fulfil their wishes. This world is full of trees. If people are praying to 'angels' because they believe they are their Gods, 'Why should I answer their prayers? I ask, 'Who am I?

I wish they could look for me to simplify their lives but they prefer to tangle them. To this tangled life, some call it enjoyment. They are blinded by illusion and it has become their God. They cannot see beyond these artificial or temporary needs. I can call everyone Kaffir (non-believers) the way everyone behaves towards me because they have forgotten me completely.

There are millions of pseudo-masters making billions of dollars and they are driving the Seekers from the proper path. Pseudo means they do not know me; otherwise, they would not commit such acts. Only a few have direct faith in me. There are many sincere and faithful people but their faith is not in me but in my representatives or prophets. They are taught to have faith in their Masters, who do not exist in this world.

Their sincerity is also not pure, it is mainly used to fulfil their desires or physical ailments. Out of this sincerity, religions are created and some temples are constructed because they believe I only exist in these places. Again, these temples are not in my name. Organizations privately or publicly own them. People go to these places to pray or look for me or feel my presence, although I live so close in their hearts. I am in each soul and everywhere.

When they go to these temples, I wonder where they are going when I am already so close. Now you know why their prayers are not answered. They depend more on their gurus or teachers. Most of these teachers don't lead their followers to look for me. Instead, they are telling them to follow their systems or traditional rituals. Any religion having or believing in a caste system, colour or race does not represent me. They are far far away from my threshold.

Regardless of how religious he may claim to be if any person acts as Master and others are his servants, he is not representing me. Each soul is individual and I have given the capability to all if they want to know me and feel my presence. I am also residing within that servant of yours and in that position. 'If you feel I am inferior, then how can you know me?

As God; 'Who am I?

All objects in the universe and infinite knowledge together know what I am. I sent all souls into the lower worlds to unfold and be aware of me. They are to learn and attain all the qualities as I do. The challenge is enormous and the mind dictates in the lower worlds and to know all this is not to mind likings. Overall, every individual feels I am beyond knowing and out of reach, so I am labelled as unknown.

I am like a good father who is humble, sincere to all his children and provides for all their needs but never has been appreciated. When a negative force (Kal) gives you less and robs you of more, it still shines in your eyes. The known has become the unknown. You make me wonder if I am in a foreign land. This is why the question arises and some ask, 'Does God exist? 'Where is God? 'Has anyone seen God?

The answers are often in silence or silenced by rude remarks or attacks. This is why new or modern thoughts arise in this world; I only believe in science or my ego. Religions have failed to represent me in the true image. There is always one Master representing me and many others who also feel my presence throughout this world. Instead of learning the spiritual way into my arms, you create religions in their names, 'prophets,' and I am pushed to the side.

All religions celebrate their saint or prophets' history, including births and deaths. During these celebrations, your thoughts travel centuries back and you dwell on that experience while relating to your guru, whether it was good or bad. But at present, you all leave me while claiming that you are searching for me. 'Can you imagine people sitting on a bus and leaving me at a bus stop, yet they have gone to see me?

Looking at these situations, a question arises, 'Who am I? All within my own house, forget me. Satnam Ji is my only true representative, the rest of them are my messengers. This is why they only express part of me. That is why there are so many religions. If all my messengers knew me as Satnam does, their message would be the same and there would have been only one religion. The difference in the message is the cause of all religious fights.

All religions claim that their guru or teacher is a prophet but they never wonder if their prophet was involved in any religious wars. At those times, he was not representing me, so, 'How can he be a prophet? My true messenger is often silent or made silent by others because no one is ready to listen or face the truth. Those who are converting others religiously are against spiritual law. They believe they are doing my will but wrong because I did not create any religions.

All religions are man-made and established for many reasons. Conversion is a clear indication of creating bad karma.

Those who are fighting religious wars are also against my wishes. There is no religion that did not fight a religious war and so all these religions are not representing me or their prophets. Those who kill in the name of religion are going far from me and are losing my love. Now it is a known factor; those who kill in the name of religion are not religious.

Even their people are saying this and condemning these acts. They are also aware that they are killing in the name of religion but in effect, they are executing their anger due to their own negative experiences in life. Those religious leaders or prophets who are killing my creation or are recommending that killing and eating of animals is normal, cannot represent me. I am responsible for feeding the whole creation. Then how can my representatives or I recommend you to eat meat?

When a person is suffering and has given up on their religion, which often fails the individual, religious leaders stress having stronger faith than helping the individual. As Jesus said once, man shall not live by bread alone. Why does this person not get any help? Because they are all spiritually inactive religions. Their Masters or gurus do not exist anymore.

The day will come when no one will answer your prayers and you will cry in vain and make a request; 'Whoever you are and wherever you are, please help me.' I will answer and help because you are part of me. I am responsible for all; your sufferings are my own because I experience your sufferings myself. I have always supported but I want you to become aware of everything consciously. At last, this person who has given up comes to one conclusion and says, 'Wherever you are, please help me, God.'

Only then does this person come in contact with my live channel or I appear in disguise. People often fail to feel my presence because they want to see me under their conditions. I am always here if you arise above your conditions, needs and thoughts. My whole creation has problems due to their own created bad karma but they often raise their hands in the air, pointing at me and asking for help. Did you ever think, 'If I have problems, to whom do I complain? I like to see everyone take responsibility for their actions and let me be as I am, just as I let you be yourself.

Spiritual travel is the only hope for the future. It means the practical side of God bringing back the souls to me. This spiritual science will prove all religions are fake and baseless and have no practical answer to any question. Eventually, people will lose their faith and walk away to practical spiritual science to experience my presence directly. All the known prophets and their names will become unknown, as I am at present.

God; 'Who am I?

EYE OF SOUL

When Seeker is searching for the truth, spiritual freedom or any esoteric experiences, several statements are given by religions or cults to attract the Seeker. The biggest attraction is soul travel, followed by light and sound, past lives, telepathy and miracles. 'What are the main points or virtues we need to look at for our success or failure? Yet we expect to do spiritual travel.

What is this point we need to look at? Our first eye is the 'third-eye.' The soul is here for schooling on the physical plane to experience. Where is the seat of the soul in the physical body? Two eyes are for our physical use and most of the illusion is seen or experienced through them. They are the leading cause of creating our karma. We often blame the mind for our wrong-doings but don't forget that our two eyes first see something and then the mind executes the situation, either to create good or bad karma in our account.

The result is based on what our two eyes have seen. It is also essential to know which mind was active, the lower or spiritual. 'Where is our first eye responsible for spiritual travel and other esoteric experiences? That is our **pineal gland,** which is known as the seat of the soul. Although it is a physical organ in the head, at the same time, it is one of the most important spiritual centre. It is known as the third-eye because we heard of it through some religious scriptures or mythological stories.

At present, it is beyond our knowledge or out of reach. Once you come to know the third-eye's presence, then you will prefer to view this world and beyond through this eye. Now you know why it is our first eye. During meditation, the answers to your problems are given through this spiritual centre and passed over to the mind and the astral body to express physical results.

How many of you pay any attention to the pineal gland's welfare when there are so many? Half of you don't even know where it is in the head, yet you believe to be serious spiritual Seekers. When you want to learn any subject, you have to learn from scratch to finish, mastering the subject. All professional sports-people condition their bodies to perform at the competition. Although we are not competing with anyone, our competition is within. So, 'What are you doing to condition yourself to accomplish your spiritual goal?

When T. E. Lawrence went to join the Great Arab Revolt as a liaison officer in 1916, he made a thorough study of that country and the nature of its people and the possible problems he was going to face. He only felt comfortable taking this task until he realised fully what he was going to be involved with. In the end, he was very successful. In the same way, we have to thoroughly study the subject of the soul, spiritual centres and their welfares.

Every person in this world knows or has heard of the word soul but simply knowing these four letters will not lead you anywhere. There are two basic welfares of the pineal gland; physical and spiritual. For the physical, if the pineal gland is not healthy, it affects the physical body and some symptoms will indicate this. Medical experts are aware of this and it is essential to eat healthy foods to activate the pineal gland.

Vegetarian food makes a lot of difference. Vegetarian food is mainly water-based, considered clean and healthy with high vibrations. It helps to keep the pineal gland healthy. Seaweed kelp found in the ocean has many nutrients (such as iodine), which is perfect for the pineal gland. Seaweed kelp also helps to fight cancer. Kelp is available in most health stores. Animals drink water and have blood in their bodies, similar to humans.

That is the difference between vegetarian and non-vegetarian foods. Because animals have blood in their bodies, 'Do you know they have their DNA? Vegetarian food is water-based or its DNA is in our favour. 'Now, can you imagine the number of DNA you added to your body within one life span? The stronger the DNA, the more you add karma to your account. After adding so much DNA to your account, surely you can imagine how healthy your spiritual side is.

I don't think your pineal gland is as active as you want to see or expect it to be. This is the answer to those who ask, 'What difference does it make? The pineal gland is the seat of the soul or the third-eye. It should be active and healthy. Spiritual travel is only possible if the pineal gland is healthy. If it is not healthy, it will not stir the positive vibrations we need before any spiritual travel is possible. If physically it is healthy, we have to tune it spiritually to keep it active all the time.

Tuning yourself spiritually is very important to materialise your goal. There are many ways you can do this. Do your spiritual exercises regularly, rely on your spiritual Master, read discourses or be given spiritual material in the shape of books and mental fast. It would help to keep your pineal gland active to do spiritual travel at any time. 'Have you prepared yourself for this experience? Or 'Did you assume it will happen because you want it to happen?

Other signs of an unhealthy pineal gland are that you will not have sound, transparent dreams or you will not remember them. This may be the answer to those who are complaining about this issue. It may not be correct if I say the Master gives you spiritual dreams but does not want you to remember them. If he does not want you to remember them, then what is the purpose of giving them to you in the first place?

Our book, 'The Will of God,' is the result of remembering all the dreams because they are given for a purpose. In very rare cases, the Master gives you the experience and only gives you a nudge that something has taken place. It is always for the benefit of the Seeker. The examples shown above are suitable for keeping your pineal gland decalcified and they will activate the gland.

The pineal gland is calcified when a lot of toxic material is built around it; as explained earlier, non-vegetarian food is not suitable. We must eat natural foods to remove this build-up of crystallised deposits. Many people prefer to drink lots of water. Do you know it brings lots of fluorides, chlorine and bromide? They all contribute to calcifying your pineal gland unless you have a water purifier system installed in your household or drink bottled water.

Most of the foods we eat are genetically modified. They are not natural, as we believe and they all contribute to toxifying this gland and are a cause of cancer in the human body. Try to purchase organic foods if possible. Other foods toxic to this gland are sugar, caffeine, alcohol, cocaine and heroin.

Smoking is the worst. We know it is toxic for our lungs and leads to cancer but it is also bad for the pineal gland.

Too many headaches or heavy heads after waking up from sleep are signs of a toxic presence. If you wake up happy and feel light-headed, that is a sign of good health. We never pay much attention to our heads apart from washing our faces, shaving or putting on make-up. 'If our skulls and other organs, too many to name, are healthy, who needs makeup? The appearance of getting old, which we usually see on everyone's face, results from what is going on within our skulls.

The whole body depends on the head. When we fail to sleep, something is making us feel uncomfortable and our nervous system is also not in harmony. Good, healthy foods and keeping spiritual vibrations high are vital to spending our lives balanced and happy. There is one experience we all have now and then. We feel a pleasant, warm sensation within the forehead area.

This happens during meditation or sometimes when we have positive thoughts during the day. It is good to have but we need to go further. Due to spiritual efforts, the third-eye becomes active, which is the seat of the soul. This activation shows that our spiritual vibrations are being stirred within the skull but we fail to go further. If you sit down, take advantage of this activation and concentrate on the pineal gland, where the soul sits calmly.

Once you feel its presence, action is required to move the soul through the Crown-Chakra. Spiritual travel is not easy as we expect it to be but experience given by the spiritual Master is effortless. It is very similar to a toy given to a child.

This child is thrilled but this child did not go to work to earn money so that this child could buy this toy with their effort. If you want to do something of your own accord, it is not that easy.

It is the same as when we often use this phrase; 'You need to become the Master of your universe.' These are beautiful words but this is how you have to materialise with your efforts. When you read about successful yogis and saints, you probably now realise that they live on less and eat natural foods. They are usually in meditation, either sitting down in a tailor fashion or mentally fasting when walking.

I can write a lot more on this subject but the question is, 'Is your eye of soul healthy and do you know where it is? Are you trying to find its existence? If you do, are you using your first eye properly to do spiritual travel? You know it is not your third-eye; it is their first eye to the spiritual people. To the others who are unaware, it is their third-eye. The pineal gland is also known as the mystery gland because this is the way to reach higher levels of consciousness while still being present in the physical body.

The pituitary gland is the seat of the mind and it is also known as the master gland. It is situated at the base of the nose and below the brain and it is very close to the optic nerve. It controls other hormone glands such as the adrenal and the thyroid. It is usually pea size and weighs about 0.5 grams. It is within a small bone cavity. It is responsible for regulating several functions in balance.

Body over or undergrown in size is due to the pituitary gland malfunction.
Blood pressure.

Balance of water within the body.
Energy.
Sex organs.
Temperature regulation.

The recommended vitamins for the pituitary gland are A, D and E.

A tumour on the pituitary gland can be responsible for headaches, fatigue and more symptoms. Vitamin E prevents oxidative damage to the pituitary gland.

The thyroid gland is situated in the neck area and controls our growth and metabolism. Two small adrenal glands sit on top of the kidneys and help us deal with our stress by releasing the hormones. As said earlier, the pituitary gland is responsible for controlling the hormones in certain glands. Now you see how important it is to look after the pituitary gland.

The following sketch clearly shows where your pituitary and pineal glands are. Study them thoroughly to see. Have you been putting your attention in the correct place all these years? Although the pineal gland is the seat of the soul or the third-eye and the pituitary gland is the seat of the mind, if you manage to stir the vibrations on either gland, the whole area within the dots becomes live. You will feel the sensation within your forehead area and the strength of your attention will indicate your success in the experience.

Such as sensation only, seeing the light, hearing sound, deep samadhi and finally, an out-of-body experience. I am sure this chapter has given you some insight into the spiritual glands to keep them healthy and most importantly, how to use them. Every soul has the right to see through this eye. We often hear statements such as, 'What is reality? Reality is only experienced through the eye of the soul when it is open. The vision of two physical eyes is an illusion. 'Will you have success?

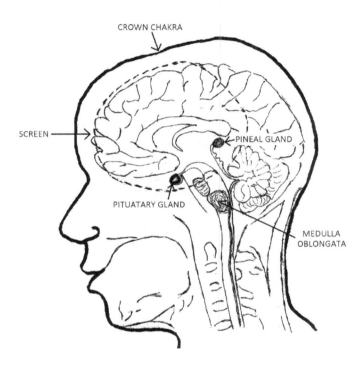

This is a replica of the Hospital X-ray to show the position of the pineal and pituitary glands. I have already given pictures of these glands in my book 'The Way to God' to appear simple to understand. These are one hundred percent correct positions, so you can master your technique to materialise a successful experience. If you find it difficult to locate them, please use your imagination to believe that you are focusing on them. Successful creativity can help stir the vibrations.

A forehead screen is used to visualise the picture of the spiritual Master. When we recommend pulling attention backward from the screen, it is because the position of these glands; otherwise, most of your effort is wasted. A successful stir of vibrations can turn the whole dotted area near the third-eye, very similar to a light in a room. Once this dotted area is spiritually enlightened, then focus on the screen. That can lead you to see the light and attention centred in the middle area (inner ears), leading you to hear the sound.

Feeling the soul's presence and gently looking up can lead the soul through the Crown-Chakra and a successful spiritual travel. One more point from the sketch is that the Crown-Chakra is not precisely on top of the pineal gland. I ask you to lift your chin slightly up; only then can the Crown-Chakra, pineal gland and spine appear in one straight line to have a successful flow of Spirit.

Make an effort and you will have success.

ART OF LIVING

You have to be an artful dodger to survive in this world. The whole world has lost this art and suffers at the hands of each other. God did not create our lives to suffer as much as we do. We must learn to live stress-free. What is the leading cause of stress? We have forgotten how to love and give impersonal love to all of God's creation. This world has become a royal rumble and everybody is fighting individually.

A famous verse 'Good of the whole' is forgotten or practiced half-heartedly. We cannot have peace unless we have stress-free minds and violence-free society. There is some kind of fear ticking within ourselves. Our leading cause of suffering is that we have forgotten how to be brave; we depend on too many people and our self-confidence is very low. Build up your stamina to be strong enough to face the world alone.

You should feel that you are the best born on this earth. When you lose your confidence, the reasons are many; personality conflict, financial status, education and body strength. Once you feel inferior to others, your suffering begins and life will be miserable. Taking responsibility in life is very important. If you are responsible for all actions taken, most things or problems will fade away. Do not expect happiness all the time; life is a mix of joy and sadness. Do not try to be too happy or too sad.

Learn to live a balanced life that way, you can avoid many hurting moments. Those who live in balance never fail in life. Those who have a habit of living happily often get hurt when dramatic situations occur in life. In marriage, people often get hurt because things are not working according to their expectations. Everyone lives in a self-created world; to live happily, we must learn to tolerate because everyone has the right to express their opinion.

We must learn to accept people as they are; things only go out of proportion when we want something to happen our way. Others' way of life could be better than yours if you have the patience and examine it thoroughly. At or before marriage, we all have fairy-tale imaginations about our partners; handsome, kind and loving. You never know what your fate has in store for you. Your world may turn upside down and a non-stop battle has begun?

All this can calm down with patience and love but our frustration exploits everything out of proportion. It is our glorious moment up to our wedding day and after that, it all becomes stress and hardships. If we create love and affection for each other, the magic in life returns. Keep that passion alive, the one you had when you met the first time. Life will bring shocking moments as it unfolds and the butterflies are still around, the ones you had seen earlier. Keep working on building that trust for each other.

Broken trust is the killer of relationships. In marriage or a social circle, we all should make an effort to build relationships. One-sided effort in any situation is not healthy; with time, everything will vanish, whether someone is a friend or in love. In one-sided friendship or love, we often get hurt. No one has won the world with violence. Love is a winner all the time. We look for compatibility in love or friendship because this is what we have learned from our families or society.

If two people are too compatible, two things can happen. They can be very successful and make themselves very big in life. Something can occur oppositely because both love to express their opinions but do not tolerate what has been said by the other, bringing catastrophic results. We must learn to give psychic space to each other. In marriage, we try to dominate our partners, it is better to live life as good friends and during hard times, we stand with each other like solid rocks.

Hardship and happiness are part of our lives. We must learn to move on in life as we progress with time; we all are in constant change. Do not hold on to the past that is history. I have often heard couples saying, 'He is not the same man I married,' or 'She is not as pretty as she used to be.' With time and responsibility, we all change. We cannot remain twenty-five forever and old age takes its toll. Do not repeat past mistakes that weaken the relationship. No one is perfect in this world.

During some quarrel, Jesus Christ said to the crowd, 'Any person who has not committed any sin should throw the stone first,' and everyone stepped back. This is the truth. People who are simple in mind and live simple lives are the happiest because they have very few demands and have nothing to gain or lose. I always believed in looking good and feeling better and people around you can see the spark in your personality.

People often ignore those who are miserable or look dull. Your character can pull people towards you like a magnet;

otherwise, everything repels you. Always learn to appreciate what you have; I always believed that before it's time or beyond your luck, you will not receive or nothing will come your way. Be satisfied with what you have. We often fail when we begin to dream that the grass is greener in the next field. We usually end up making mistakes and losing what we have.

Those looking better often suffer in silence without giving away any hint to anyone. You will find many brown spots in all the green fields. Be grateful for what you have. We are part of a rat race in life, trying to get wealthy or good status, being better than the people we know. This also brings misery when you fail. A negative attitude makes a big hole in your aura or persona, things begin to fade away and you lose what you already had.

My approach to life is different. What God has given me already is above average; I am not super rich or poor, so 'Why should I complain? Be satisfied with what you have; you will always be happy. You can find happiness in flowers. Otherwise, millions of pounds cannot make you happy. Every person is a hero in their way. You have the confidence and God has given you common sense. Be in command of your life. We fail when someone pulls our strings and brings misery into our lives.

Some people will be jealous in many ways and try to harm you and in return, you may hold grudges. This could be a silent killer because it will affect your mind and health. Learn to forgive and leave them alone. If you don't retaliate, they will move somewhere else to feed their harmful habit. Be happy all the time and you will never grow old; wrinkles on your face result from stress. Honesty is the key to a happy and healthy life.

At work, be honest with the task you have been given and do enough work to earn your living. Never forget that someone is paying you for each minute, hour or day. Live your life actively and honestly. Laziness is responsible for poor health and stress. A few minutes of exercise can save your day. Live your day so that it is your last day in this world and you will make the most of it.

Respect and appreciate all life; you will get abundant love in return. We all are social creatures. If you are not strong enough to live alone, then have a circle of friends who will be there when you need them. Help others as much as you can because it will give you pleasure. No one is perfect. Do not try to find faults in others. Self-analysis is important because it could be you at fault. Have a unique goal in life apart from your regular work or family.

At the end of your life, you can say, 'Yes, I have achieved this.' Otherwise, you will be a person like any other who came and went without a trace. Make your mark in this world. Keep moving towards your set goal and be focused. Failures will be many but never give up. It is this hunger within that keeps you alive and strong. God sent souls on earth to learn. The physical body is given to express itself and execute its learning actions so learn as much as possible.

Keep moving and with time, you will mature. We cannot remain children, all our lives. Moving and travelling are essential. You cannot know the whole world standing in one place or living in the same house. The entire world is waiting for you to explore. Taking risks is important because it will build your stamina and self-confidence. Otherwise, life is slipping through your fingers every day. We often fail by saying, 'I cannot do this.'

There will be so many who want to see you fail in life. However, we often fail ourselves. Time is necessary and every minute counts, so don't sleep like junk on the heap; make the most of your day. Then you can say, 'Today, I have done this or that.' Live your life as an example to others. Dive into the sea of life to find pearls. Hold lots of love within until you become the magnet of love. Then you don't need to find love because everyone is attracted to you and the choice will be yours.

Don't search for love, be the creator of love. You can bring magic to many people's lives. Divorce is only for people who are dominating, non-tolerant, bored or unserious in life. Hold on to the smile on your face because it can make someone's day. If you suspect something is wrong, learn to say no; otherwise, it can bring misery to your life. You don't have to drag your life when you can run on roller skates.

Don't feel empty in life. Fill each corner of your life to experience and let people feel awe, saying, 'How did you do it? If you have committed a mistake somewhere in life, undo the situation or learn to say sorry. Sometimes it is better to have or make a blunt statement now rather than telling hundreds of lies later. Never expect rewards for your good deeds; it can lead to depression.

A person who was suffering from depression went to see a doctor. The doctor gave him several medicines and recommended a few other therapies but nothing worked.

In the end, he suggested watching a very famous circus in that area to this patient. The joker of this circus was very famous for making people laugh. The doctor was sure it should work. This patient replied, 'I am that joker.' Then the doctor asked this patient, 'In your opinion, who do you think is the biggest joker? The patient pointed his thumb up towards the sky, meaning God.

God is responsible for the whole creation and it is very similar to any circus. According to God, it has created everything equal and opposite, in proportion to keep a perfect balance. God thought of each soul's survival and provided all means of living and feeding natural herbs to fight against any disease. The five passions of our mind are driving us in different directions. We are full of greed, ego and the desire to be more powerful than anyone else.

God created this land of happiness but we are never satisfied because we received everything easy and free. This is why we do not appreciate what we have received. The five passions of our mind are deadly when abused; if they are in balance, then the same five passions can bring many spices into our lives to enjoy. That is their purpose in the first place. All lower lives are living according to nature and are happy.

Did you ever see any bird or animal going to see the doctor on its own or going to a shopping centre? The answer is no. They follow the dictates of God and are living happily. Mind you, all wildlife receives food daily without fail. 'Do you know why? Because they trust the joker within. All domestic pets, such as dogs and cats, are more likely to get sick than wild ones and we take them to the veterinarian for treatment to make them feel better.

Do you know why they get sick? Because they are imprisoned within four walls, similar to humans. Be yourself and let the others be. Live your life in the name of God. It will take care of all your needs. Vacuum all materials from life and fill it up with Spirit.

This is the art of living.

THE WHEEL OF 84

In the beginning, we should know the number of God's creations. According to old Hindu religious texts, there are approximately 3 million plant species, 2.7 million insect species, 1.4 million bird species, 0.9 million sea species and 0.4 million land animals. The total is 8.4 million or 84 lakh incarnations and above all, others are humans, angels and demons.

As humans, we are always concerned about our well-being. 'First, we should know what we are? The physical body is known as Pinda, which means one day it is bound to die or be destroyed in one way or the other. The word Pinda is from the Hindu language and means the human body. This Pinda is known as the genetic entity (GE), which is made of natural chemicals. It is an oxygen machine that dies naturally, accidentally or intentionally. It is used by the soul as a shell for a temporary basis during each incarnation.

The process of death on a natural basis is as follows. The soul leaves the body and enters into the next life. The soul usually exits at the pineal gland and finds its way through the Crown-Chakra but not always. The person with a lower consciousness, the soul, can leave through any one of the psychic chakras. This is the case for most humans today.

Our medical science has proved that numbness begins to creep up the feet area near natural death, gradually moving higher along the body until it reaches the heart. Then heart stops due to a lack of blood circulation. The soul is free like a bird to fly or be escorted by the angels. The soul breaks the silver cord with the clay shell it has used for several years. No physical pain is experienced.

Any natural death is no more painful than birth. The silver cord is still attached between the astral, causal, mental and soul body. The astral body will represent the soul in the court of the lord of karma, not the soul as many believe. It is very similar to the physical body representing us on this plane. Souls with heavy karmic patterns leave through the lower chakras of the spine instead of the natural means through the third-eye.

After death, the only growing thing left is the nails and hairs if the body is kept for a few days or until it begins to decay. During natural death, the angels appear to escort the soul to the Astral Plane in the court of the lord of karma. He is always in court to take care of all newcomers. As most religious texts describe, there is no sitting in some jail cell.

After judgement, he draws the curtain over your past life's memories so that you can accept the new incarnation and its conditions of living as the will of God without questioning. One in a million may remember a past life. Although there are several sections to accommodate everyone, there is a waiting period of a minimum of seventy-two hours or it could be many years if the soul's exact karma does not match for future learning.

If the minimum karma is left, all souls do not come back to this earth. Then they are given a chance to proceed to higher planes. All religions stress that birth in human form is significant. God has gifted the soul with the awareness of all other bodies, which actively helps the soul shed all karma on all planes at once, directly proceed to the soul plane and achieve spiritual freedom. After finishing karma on the physical plane, the death process is enacted upon every plane.

We are in the Astral Plane and work out our karma according to that plane. The astral body has to be dispersed there and move in the court of the causal plane. There, the causal body will represent the soul for the judgement and the lord of that plane will decide the future incarnation on the Astral Plane. Alternatively, you may proceed to the mental or the soul plane.

Most religious followers do not follow their respected religions for many reasons or do not take them seriously. The fear of death and future consequences in heaven and hell regarding their wrong-doings is pumped into their brains by the priests. This is the calculated formula of previous saints, who knew that humans are the only creatures of God who are always aggressive towards God's ways. Instead of submitting and adjusting to God's ways, humans always calculate how to outsmart God's ways and get nature's best.

People believe or are misled by priests that you will be tortured in many ways or dropped in fire or put in boiling oil. All these statements lead to one conclusion; that you have been punished for your wrong-doings. It also means that now you have become karma-less. If that is the case, 'How can you have another incarnation on earth? At the same time, they also point out you are coming back to the world for the next incarnation.

They are all contradictory to their statements because none have any practical experience in this field; they simply pass on information heard from somewhere. When people hear the name of Jam-Dutes (Angels of Death), it brings fear to all. They do not know who these souls are. Dharam-Raj (King of dead) is the head of this responsibility. Dharam means religion, the person who acts as the true righteous of justice and he does not waver from his actual duty. He is also known as Yama.

His assistants are known as Dutes. Dutes means ministers, very similar to our physical parliament. They are called Yam-Dutes, which means people or angels sent by Dharam-Raj to escort the soul to its court. 'Therefore, how can they mistreat any person? Death is the beginning of true life in God's world. It is known that death is only an illusion; then, there is little need for you to have a cause of fear. Priests only create this fear.

Yama is also known as self-discipline and there is another interpretation for this; not killing any creation of God and living life as directed by God. This is the death procedure of ordinary people but the Master directly escorts those who follow God's messenger to their earned spiritual plane. The true Master always guides the followers to set their minimum goal; it should be Self-realisation but you can achieve God-realisation in this life.

BIG BROTHER IS WATCHING

In life, we try to get away with almost anything we can. This is how our families or society has trained us. If not, sometimes our circumstances force us to follow the path of deception; as the saying goes, everything is fair in love or war. Though they are religious, most people ignore the ethics of their beliefs. They believe if no one is looking, they can get away with it. First of all, you always know whether your actions are negative or positive.

It does not matter if you are aware of your actions but you should know that Big Brother is always watching you. Now you may be wondering, 'Who is this Big Brother? It is God; who always nudges within to make you aware of your actions. You are always mindful of your actions and you can ignore the whole world but you cannot overlook within. This overlooking is the cause of your suffering. It is known as karma.

Once there was a saint. He decided to choose his successor from his followers in his old age. There were only two deserving disciples, in his opinion. He thought I'd better test them to see who is more sincere to God. Saint had two speaking parrots. During ancient times, this was a tested and tried method; he called both and gave them the same task to follow. The saint handed them one parrot each and said, 'Kill these parrots where you think no one is looking or watching you.'

The one who comes back first will be eligible to take my place. Both walked away. The first disciple looked around and thought no humans were looking; he began to break the neck of the parrot. The parrot spoke; I am looking, I am looking. He did not listen to the spiritual message and broke the neck of his parrot and killed it. He came back to his teacher. Master, I have killed it where no one was watching or looking at us, so I have come back first. For his second disciple, they waited for a long time.

After a long time, he returned with the live parrot in his hands. The first disciple was happy and thought he was the winner. The saint asked his second disciple, 'How come you did not kill your parrot? The disciple answered, 'I went everywhere and no humans were looking but God was watching. Then I went inside a dark room so no one could see us but my inner state of consciousness was looking.

The parrot did not speak this time because he knew Big Brother was watching. This is why it took me so long to return. He realised that Big Brother was watching him everywhere. The saint was pleased with his answer and chose him as his successor. I have two bird feeders in my garden and it's lovely to see birds eat seeds. Sometimes it is fascinating to watch them.

On average, fifty to one hundred parrots turn up daily and their routine is to sit directly on the birdfeed cage. Others only pick up what has been dropped on the ground by parrots. A few magpies, sparrows, two robins, two pigeons and three doves attend daily. Squirrels play their games to steal. There is always a rivalry between pigeons and doves. The pigeons always chase away the doves so they cannot eat whatever is dropped on the ground by parrots.

When pigeons are not around, there is one dove bigger in size than the other two and she chases the small doves maybe forty feet away and then comes back to eat. But all of them have the same aim; to fill up their bellies. It gives me pleasure to watch them but at the same time, I notice their behaviour of cheating and domination. Good luck to them. I do not interfere, it is a law of nature. But at the same time, they are not aware that Big Brother is watching their misdeeds.

In the animal kingdom, there is jungle law. Hunters can claim whatever they spot, grab and kill. We begin with lions and tigers because they are the strong pack. For example, they manage to kill buffalo. Then many hyenas arrive and they always come in big numbers. They irritate the lion pack so that the lions leave their kill and hyenas eat the feast. 'Now the question arises, who is the sinner?

This is what most people think, 'We did not kill; we only eat that which was already killed or dead.' We follow this in steps. **First:** the farmer raises his animal stock for slaughter purposes. **Second:** animals are led to the slaughter machine. **Third:** the drivers transport meat to the shops or stores. **Fourth:** butchers at the meat shop cut the meat into small pieces for selling purposes. **Fifth:** people buy the meat, will clean and cook it to eat.

But this last person thinks he is not responsible. Do not forget that you are the last person to dispose of the animal body by eating it. Did you notice the whole procedure is in five steps? The circle is complete and none of these five people had any pity for the animals. Now we follow this from a different viewpoint. 'For whom did the farmer raise his animal stock? 'For whom was the animal killed? 'For whom was it transported? 'For whom was the meat cut into pieces? 'Who went to the shop willingly to buy meat?

As I said, we humans always have a habit of self-denial of any wrongdoing. If this last person (the customer) were not available, the whole procedure would have never occurred. So, you don't decide how responsible you are for this act. It is the job of Big Brother, who is always watching you.

No one can deceive Big Brother.

BLACK MAGIC

Black magic is one of the deadliest, scariest and most dangerous occupational hazards. Occupational means these black magicians do not provide this service for free. They are fully trained people and a few pretend to be black magicians, they are known as pseudo-masters and naive people are robbed of their money with no service provided. In Asian countries like India and Pakistan, there is a big demand for these practitioners.

The sad part is, when these people moved into European countries or other parts of the world, this negative practice also travelled with them. The root cause of this practice is jealousy. 'Now, the question is, who wants to harm you? You are very proud of the people better known as your near and dear family. The large population of this world doesn't know who you are and what you do or don't do; they have no concern. The very close people know what you do and watch you like a hawk.

If you are poor and suffering, most are happy; one or two may be concerned and try to help you. The behaviour of these people is based on their upbringing. This is what they have learned from parents or their society. Any person who finds success with hard work or becomes successful overnight, I don't think that it is much appreciated in the close circle. They may pretend to congratulate you but their minds have devious schemes to bring you down from your throne.

When nothing works, they approach black magicians. You may be wondering, 'How can you find these people? It is so simple. Most Asian newspapers are full of adverts by these people. I said earlier that out of these advertisements, some are genuine and many are pseudo. When any person is suffering, they are willing to approach anyone who claims to be a practitioner of black magic and they are willing to pay for this service.

What is black magic? It is the use of evil spirits for evil purposes and to harm others. It is considered a dark art because it is used to control or harm others who are irritating your mind in many ways. To this art, people give different names such as black magic, sorcery, witchcraft, occult practice and more. Those involved in this practice, if they feel that you or someone else is crossing their path, then they will create obstacles in your life.

Black magic is sent through certain postulates of evil spirits to the person to be harmed. Once you become a black magician, there is no turning back. Some charge a small fee while others charge a large amount of money. It depends on your reputation. Apart from earnings, you are creating bad karma for yourself at the cost of people's suffering by your wrong-doing. The person who hired you for this purpose is also bound to suffer.

I don't think both parties can pay it back that easily. You may feel happy to see someone suffering at the hands of your wrong-doing but it will all backfire on you one day. I have come across some black magicians throughout the years. At the end of their life span and near death, they physically suffered. The lord of karma makes sure these people suffer; he does not spare anyone and does not stop anyone from this negative practice.

God has given free will to all souls to live their lives as they wish. White magicians aim to help others, undo negative spells and bring peace and justice to the people who approach them. Black magic is used for many reasons. They use this practice to control someone in love, communicate with wandering souls or control someone as an enslaved person. To achieve immortality is their belief but it cannot be done through negative force.

'I don't think many of these practitioners know what true spiritual freedom is? Black magicians consider the outcome of what their customer wants to see and several rituals can be used for different purposes. Black magicians rarely visit the customer's house to practice unless something in the house is disturbing and has to be seen and dealt with there and then.

Usually, black magicians have built a system in their living place and all the required equipment is at hand because they use some items to bring the result. They use candles, herbs, crystals and costly perfumes to attract the entities. They also have harmful items such as dolls and needles. These needles are used on dolls to send pain to the person to be harmed while reciting black magic or spell. They poke needles into the doll, believing that this is the person involved in the suffering.

This victim will suffer at a successful attempt and distance is no problem. People in India send this kind of wrong-doing to England, Canada and the rest of the world. Sometimes one attempt is enough; otherwise, it is repeated several times to get the result for their customers and send misery to those considered enemies. Most of the time, the victims are innocent, decent and down-to-earth people but the way you look at them, they appear to be your enemy.

Sometimes black magicians or the person who wants to hurt someone gets into trouble. If the opposite person holds a high state of consciousness, his aura act as a mirror. Whatever is sent to the person often reflects the sender and then the black magician and the customer receive their own medicine, not knowing how this can be. When using these dark forces, the practitioner must be careful, fully trained and control the situation.

When these forces are used naively, these dark forces can backfire on the doer and can become insane. Several people end up in mental hospitals and treatment given by regular doctors will not work. A small mantra (magic) can end their misery in minutes or hours. Some people have a moderate physical disability and believe someone does black magic. They are innocent people who end up in the wrong hands and give away their livelihood for no reason.

Despite their efforts, physical ailment still exists. Sometimes when things are not working according to their plans in life, some people take it as black magic on them. It is not always true and sometimes, these troubles arrive at your doorstep due to self-created bad karma. All suffering is not black magic and these black magicians are no friends to anyone; they are only interested in your money.

In India, expert black magicians use graveyards to trap new entities. People in India use pyres to burn corpses.

The pyre is assembled by stacking some amounts of wooden pieces, the corpse is placed on top and the ritual is to set fire by their loved ones. It takes a few hours to burn the corpse and then it takes a few hours to cool the ashes or remains of the body. The next day, family members go back to the graveyard and pick up unburned bones, nails, etc.

These black magicians go there at midnight to pick up the skull if it is fully intact. In most cases, the skull is broken into small pieces with heat. They believe that with the help of the skull, they can control the deceased person's soul by performing some ritual and this soul can be used as a ghost to harm others. This ghost can be sent to disable someone physically as long as this ghost is within the body. I have been through this myself.

Someone I knew, a family member in India, was unhappy with me. I was in my room in England and one day, I suddenly felt a jerk as if someone had entered my body. My head area was normal but my body action was similar to being lazy and I did not want to lift a finger to do anything. My body was disabled, even though I am a very energetic person. I gave it some thought for a day or two and pictured the involved person who wanted to harm me.

I did not hesitate to phone him and I warned him to go to the person he hired for this job. Otherwise, I will send the same treatment back to him and his practitioner. He did not admit any wrongdoing but I told him to go back to the practitioner and undo it. Within a few hours, I was back to normal. Now I knew who the culprit was. This can happen to any spiritual person when one's spiritual armour is not entirely on or some weakness in the aura.

If you know someone close to you and believes in this practice, do not cross their path and try to stay away. It does not matter how close a loved one they are. To you, these people are relations but due to some reason, they consider you as their enemy. When reciting a psychic ritual, the practitioner has single-pointed attention. He does not want or like any interference, which acts as a divided focus and will not bring the expected results.

Practitioners summon the ghost, demon or entity and command it to enter the victim's aura. The practitioner fully controls these entities but they can also harm the practitioner due to negligence. These entities are no friends to anyone and at times, they can be very annoyed because they are trapped and unable to leave this world or communicate with loved ones to get help. One can imagine their frustration.

It is very easy for the people who want to harm you if they can take something that belongs to your body; hair, nails or any worn clothing (because the sweat of your body is still on the shirt). They all act as DNA to easily find your aura. Many use this practice in court cases to win over opponents. Some people do not believe in black magic but in scientific evidence. It is an individual choice what to believe.

I have seen many people fall on their backs by taking this practice lightly. Black magic practitioners could also act as white magic practitioners when a suffering person turns up at their doorsteps to get help. Practitioners can scan the problem and know what ritual to perform to undo the negative effect or spell. These practitioners are no friend to anyone; you pay them money to reverse the magic back to the sender. These practitioners are very lonely people and no one wants to be friends with them because of their reputation.

They are not to be trusted. Only devious people hang around them and they hold negative ideas. Some skilled practitioners use clay pots (Kujji practice) to kill someone. They charge a large sum of money for this ritual. They prepare the small clay pot, probably a diameter of six to seven inches and it is full of needles placed in a particular order. With the ritual, this clay pot begins to rise above the ground, fly and spin at a very high speed in the air to the destined person (victim).

When it reaches the victim, it hits their body with full force and all the needles get stuck in the body. This person is killed on the spot. During this ritual, the whereabouts of the victim must be known. If the victim is not there, this clay pot will return to the sender (practitioner), who is killed on the spot instead. Some families have property or financial claims. They are greedy and make sure all property must be theirs by hook or crook.

It occurs between brothers when one is innocent and the other is crafty. After the wedding, a newly arrived bride in the family trusts everyone and eats or drinks whatever is offered by family members. This greedy person will approach a black magician to make barren the womb of this bride. Black magicians give something to mix in the food or drink; The lady will never have a child in her whole life.

These practitioners are charging small amounts of money and someone's life is destroyed forever. 'How can one remove black magic spells? They can be removed from your body if you hold positive energy within yourself and leave no space for the entity to live. Sit in meditation and chant the word Haiome for a good twenty minutes. Visualise the white light entering your Crown-Chakra and flowing within all over so that you are full of white light.

At the same time, visualise black energy leaving your body and command it not to enter again. 'In the name of God, do not enter again.' Quit by saying, 'May the blessings be.' Repeat this a few times to get the desired results. You will find information on protecting yourself from them in my writings but sometimes, followers do not read my spiritual writings thoroughly.

CONSCIOUSNESS

State of consciousness is a widespread word amongst spiritual Seekers and religious groups. God means the total consciousness of the whole eternity and we all are trying to experience part of it and feel blessed. Absolute consciousness includes all the spiritual planes, the total void, every creature and every particle or atom. Once, our great Master said creation does not exist in you or me but we have the power of creating to experience God's presence.

People often mention 'my' or 'your' state of consciousness. I will say the success of any Seeker depends upon what you can create within yourself, with your effort consciously. It determines up to which spiritual plane you can travel or within. That will be your state of consciousness; otherwise, it is all make-believe. According to our state of consciousness, we express ourselves to the outer world and we are judged by people accordingly.

To live in the pure or highest state of consciousness, we must act in purity. God is the first cause; all others are second so that you can become Spirit. Satnam Ji is the most excellent guru appointed by God. He holds the second state of consciousness after God; the rest of the Masters or souls are third or fourth in line. Saints are those who hold a high state of consciousness and yet strive further into the higher planes.

There is always a plus element but we should achieve the highest state of consciousness we possibly can. It was inspiring to know that this saint was the sun god in the olden days, especially in Egypt or India. We see the sun is only another planet and all planets orbit it. Similarly, there is the worship of the moon in India and uncountable mythological stories. We know it is only a satellite to provide light on the earth.

God is the macrocosm and it expresses its presence through each microcosm. But to experience it on the physical plane is often distorted because of the mind and our emotions. The only way to know or understand is to dwell in this state of consciousness. This dwelling within is the art of separating the soul from the physical and mental senses. As life unfolds with time, we must grow spiritually within or near to it every day.

You should not depend on religion to solve your problems or ask for prosperity. You are in command to write your destiny. People often ask, 'Where is God? Now you are in this position where you cannot take your mind off God. You are always in communication with God. In this consciousness, the repetition of spiritual sound is continuous within. In this state, who wants to communicate with the outer world.

You have become one with Spirit. If you tell people what is happening within, they may think you are insane because it is beyond their knowledge. In this consciousness, spiritual food, also known as God's energy, is available. This way, you do not require any physical food apart from eating for formality to please others. The Master speaks with authority on divine wisdom because God has given him the spiritual mantle.

He is God-realised and holds tremendous love for his creation. He is the true guru and light bearer for this world. This is why people often call him a true saint. Whoever holds this spiritual mantle in the lower worlds means he is the only person who can have the highest state of consciousness. Although he holds this title, there is not an iota of excitement about it. Precious gems, gold, silver or coins do not attract.

He is always in peace within because he is constantly dwelling in the spiritual fountain. These Masters are always appointed by God and the first personification of God. The present Master gathers as many souls as he possibly can so they can free themselves from the wheel of eighty-four. All the status people hold in this world; such as doctors, scientists, teachers or thieves, are only different states of consciousness.

It results from the guidance we received since childhood from our parents, society or karma. This is the difference in lower or higher states of consciousness. We can reach or work towards God-realisation but maintaining that state of consciousness is a big responsibility. If we can keep this state of living, we can consider ourselves living the lives of saints. It is a continuous effort at the inner via spiritual exercises or contemplating spiritual principles.

Also, your outer form must express the inner spiritual fountain. In the beginning, we try to achieve a higher state of consciousness and eventually, it becomes a habit to dwell within a spiritual fountain. It takes a long time to realise or it comes to our attention that we have achieved what we strived for. To know the whole truth, we must experience the supreme state of consciousness. This is only possible when you are so close to God, alone.

Now the question is, 'Are we capable of doing that? In this state of consciousness, you may be lonely but not alone. You are full of love and your face's countenance will reflect the world. In this state of consciousness, you become the law unto yourself. The difference between this world and other spiritual planes is the state of consciousness. Those close to alone often say, 'My kingdom is not of this world,' or 'I live in it but am not part of it.'

When you are the Master of your universe, you will have little conscience towards any religion's social virtues, values or ethics. All these social values are the basis for all priests controlling the masses. You are free from social bondage, which is very healthy for the soul and the key to physical longevity. Do not let yourself entangle with the social laws of any lower planes. In this way, you will not succeed on the higher planes.

This is why it is important to keep your state of consciousness within the spiritual world. Your state of consciousness makes you the Master of your universe and the captain of your destiny if you can maintain it. Your good karma has led you to have a natural craving to enter the worlds beyond your physical senses. Your spiritual success cannot be gained by imitating any successful spiritual traveller. It can be achieved by the right effort and action with good deeds.

One day you will realise you are the image of God but clothed in rags and begging about everything in this world. Rightfully everything is yours, but the way you have been brought up, you have become the beggar. The realisation comes that only you have been holding yourself back from becoming the Master of your universe.

To have success, good ethics are needed but they hardly play any part. It's the same with spiritual writings; they are only booster points, but spiritual exercises and the assistance of a spiritual traveller are a must to have any success. Ethics play an excellent part in cleansing the mind and preparing you to knock on the inner door. As the door opens, you experience the spiritual world. The way they are cannot be explained in any religious scriptures.

The key to maintaining your state of consciousness is your Crown-Chakra. It is known by many names, soft spot or narrow is the way. As long as our soft spot is open, the Spirit can flow from above to within. This is only possible when we are reciting our naam or word regularly. The more you can do this; the more Spirit will flow. Most saints can maintain their consciousness due to this opening, whereas all priests depend on book knowledge.

We often go to the saints to receive spiritual blessings. Being in the presence of a good saint and his state of consciousness also benefits us. It is always better to stay close to good people who have positive attitudes and lead highly ethical lives. We are representing God on earth. We are the instruments of God and the Spirit flow through us. It is this flow that maintains the balance in the lower worlds.

This is why we are known as the chosen people. It has become our responsibility to keep this spiritual flow as much as possible. That is only possible when we maintain our state of consciousness as high or pure as possible. If you are the chosen people, then it is guaranteed that you will never have to come back into the lower worlds. Without following the living Master of the time, you will never achieve this spiritual status.

Once you dwell in the higher spiritual worlds, you become the law unto yourself. We can make our own decisions, which are always based on our spiritual experiences. That will supersede all regulations which are man-made to mental satisfaction, also known as physical justification. Any action can be justified on the physical, known as punishment but the individual still has to face the lord of karma.

All these wrong-doings and crimes committed result from physical or man-made laws. If people abide by spiritual laws, they will understand the responsibility of karmas being committed. Some religions do not believe in reincarnation or karma, so 'What can they teach their followers? This is why they openly hold holy wars and claim to be religious. We all have five bodies and they should live in a very balanced state.

Any person who is not in balance, especially the emotional body, can lead us away from our real selves and goals. The more our souls can express freely, the better state of consciousness will be maintained. This is where most religious people fail; they always express the knowledge of their holy writings but they fail to express their spiritual state of consciousness. I don't think they know the difference; it is beyond their knowing.

The subconscious mind is similar to our present-day computer system, where all our informative files are stored, even the ones we have forgotten. Only a few dreams can be remembered but the memory of every single dream or any instance in life is stored naturally. This is why some visions appear before us and something reminds us, 'Yes, I knew this before.' How do you know that you hold this higher God-consciousness?

It is similar to a fish because it cannot survive without water. You are always in communication with Spirit. People often ask, 'Where is God? I wonder sometimes and ask myself, 'Is it true that they don't know where God is and cannot feel its presence? How can this be possible? Most of them are so religious and if they cannot contact or feel God's presence, then I believe they must be knocking on the wrong door.

Physical or material sacrifices we make for Spirit are nothing but in return; what God gives you is an abundance of love and there is no comparison. What I have written in this chapter, all those proud of their religions never can. There is only one God and all religions and countries are walls between them and God. Remove these walls and walk into the arms of God. God is always waiting for your return as a spiritual assistant.

I am rephrasing an earlier statement but religious people often talk about their state of consciousness. The question is, 'What is your state of consciousness? The soul has the power to create and the whole of creation is within us and outside us. It is also true that the whole creation does not exist in you or me.

A successful spiritual traveller can open up within and the whole creation of God and its spiritual planes can be visited internally or externally. 'How successful are you in opening up and how far can you go? That will be your state of consciousness. If you cannot do either, you are no better than any person you know. This creative part will act as your yardstick to measure your success.

CREATION

Creation is a vast subject and beyond us knowing, unless you are a spiritual traveller. There is a vast difference between spiritual knowingness and the findings of science. The word of God created the whole creation. The world of creation is finished for the lower worlds. The original is within each soul to become spiritually aware of its existence and find its way back to its creator. We can be aware of God's creation but not entirely of our creator.

Ancient proverb, 'The son wouldn't know his father's birth.' All religions try to express themselves according to their knowledge but I think it is all guesswork. I do not personally support the theory of evolution. To me, it is a make-believe theory. Scientists are trying to guess the time factor by man-made equipment, which is a total waste. It astonishes me that all scholars of this world or well-known educated people agree that the whole of God's creation is original but not humans.

For example; a cow is a cow and a parrot is a parrot but we question our originality. Most of the world population believes we have progressed from a monkey species. The donkey is a replica of a horse; let me know in the future when the donkey has become the horse. I hope you got the point. We are also known to be superior and above the rest of God's creation. God created the system to run this system. God created nine 'Super Souls' to look after all the universes.

The living Master is here to give a message to all souls, ready to go back to their heavenly homes.

That is, the soul plane and Satnam Ji is responsible for each soul. All the creation flowing out of God was carried through this first manifestation of God. Although all souls are created in Anami-Lok, each soul is a manifestation of God to experience. That is why it is a known factor that God is the creator and sufferer; he is the king and pauper at the same time. God is the experience and the experiencer at the same time.

The whole of creation is an expression of God, so whoever addresses anything in the universes is God speaking to itself. This puzzles the normal human mind; 'How can that be? God created the higher planes, which are invisible and their existence is in a beingness state, beyond matter, energy, space and time. There is no action or reaction, day or night. Here is total brilliance and these planes exist in a still position, which means they do not orbit. It just is.

They are created as flat surfaces. It was important to create Satnam Ji to represent itself as the first personification so that all created souls could communicate or see God in this way. Otherwise, no one can see God, although it can be communicated through divine light and sound. Under the supervision of Satnam Ji, all lower worlds were created and so were the respective lords. Brahma, Vishnu and Shiva are responsible for creating, preserving and destroying the physical bodies after the completion of each experience.

These three are responsible for maintaining balance in this world. The soul is pure because it is part of God but naive in nature or an inexperienced soul. The soul is pure but to experience its actual ability, it is given four lower bodies to create a puzzle or maze. In the beginning, all below the soul plane was a big void; only the Spirit existed.

It was peaceful, calm and silent, with dim light appearing from above planes. The mental, causal, astral planes were created and finally, earth with light and sound in the shape of the globe. It was called the Pinda world; Pinda means the human body. All lower Worlds became subject to matter, energy, space and time. The Spirit began to plant the cosmic eggs of life forms.

The world was nurtured with natural beauty; water, greenery, fire and oxygen to accommodate human life. Higher worlds are peaceful and blissful, yet there was spiritual immaturity in all souls. God decided to create lower worlds in the shape of learning schools for all souls. Satnam, Sohang, Ramkar, Omkar and Jot-Niranjan are respective lords. Brahma, Vishnu and Shiva act as Kal power to block the floodgates and make sure that each soul is fully experienced to be an assistant in the world of being.

These lower worlds are physical, astral, causal and mental planes. The lord of the mental plane is responsible for creating the causal plane and the lord of the causal plane is responsible for creating the astral plane. The lord of the astral plane is responsible for creating the earth or physical plane. Earth is controlled by the astral plane and that is why all religions talk about hell and heaven, the king of the dead, ghosts, angels and more.

All lower planes were created spiritually and materially with light and sound to nurture them forever. Nine Super Souls make sure that all of these planes run in balance. There are several other planets and millions of stars on earth and there is space between each. This space has no existence; it is almost nothing but a space filled with spiritual energy. We only experience the fact of space once an object moves from A to B or C.

It is the same with time unless we measure or experience the events. According to Hindu Vedas (religious books), in the beginning, when the planet earth was capable of receiving the human life form, God sent its first five princes. They were very close to God and were given the responsibility to guide the future souls arriving on earth. You may call them the first five saviours. The life span of these people was many thousands of years and my spiritual finding or creation of God goes in line with Hindu Vedas.

As many believe, we came into this world as humans and did not walk on four legs. We are created in the image of Satnam Ji and this is what he looks like. Nowadays, science knows that it takes millions of years before any planet is liveable. This physical planet will become barren land incapable of supporting human life in four hundred thousand years. 'Do you know that the next world to accommodate new souls already exists?

I made a forecast in 2012 that it was going to be a new planet to receive new souls but not as believed by most religions. At the end of this span, this physical plane will be empty for the same amount of four Yugas, known as Maha-Yuga. All the remaining souls will be put into a deep sleep or sit in a bliss state until the Spirit makes this planet liveable again. Nothing of the kind is going to happen. This planet will become abandoned land similar to other planets, full of gases such as carbon monoxide.

At present, all scientists worldwide are creating all kinds of nuclear weapons and later, they will fall into the wrong hands. People will destroy this world and be incapable of supporting life like on other planets. At present, Mr Kim Jong-un of North Korea and Mr Donald Trump of the United States threaten each other with nuclear powers and most Islamic states. One day someone will be responsible for the world's destruction.

NASA and others are trying to find other planets to support life but that is wasting time. In the past, all these planets were physical worlds one at a time. There lived all forms of life very similar to this world but their advancement in science led to destruction one day. There are terrible gases and no human life can be found but it is possible to find some remains (skeletons). On 22 February 2017, a new planet was found three times the size of this planet. This will be the future physical world.

One of our religions states that God created this earth in six days and rested on Sunday. I wondered many times. Today's science proves them wrong. When God created the world, the name of days was non-existent. Although God can create the universes within seconds, it did not happen that way. All our religions are the same and most is mythology compared to reality. Mythology attracts the mind, which wants to know the truth.

Creation does not exist in you or me but God has designed this creation system so that all souls can create a partial or whole universe. God is a big circle and each soul has its small circle. You are within the circle of God; at the same time, God is also within your circle and so is the whole creation. You are within the circle of every other soul too.

There is a big circle and all circles are within circles; that is the riddle.

The whole of creation is within yourself and with spiritual ability, you can create whatever you desire. The technique is to use your imagination in meditation and postulate to create and then everything will appear on your screen. All saints have expressed that God is within each soul, better known as the state of consciousness. You can see part of the experience of God once your soul awakens.

Many people ask, 'Where is God? For example, the sun's rays on the earth prove the sun's existence. The sun's ray is not the sun but simply a projection of its substance. It is sustained by the sun. The soul on earth is a projection of the essence of God and the soul is sustained by it. Another example is the whole tree is contained in the seed and it requires time to transform itself into a visible shape or tree.

In the same way, God and all its universes are sitting within each soul but with the experience, we have to become aware of them. The awareness we have will indicate whether we are Self or God-realised people. Light and sound are the means of its projection and Spirit is food for the well-being of souls. At the end of a life span, the soul waits around in the Astral Plane till another child's body is available in the physical; the karma of that family tree should match this soul to work out for further learnings.

The soul is transferred to another field of action by taking this new life and the karma account goes with it. No soul can detach itself from its accounts until they are settled. These accounts of previous lives are stored in the causal body. When they become neutral, man or woman can be freed from lower worlds to enter into God's world of being and become mini-Gods, known as assistants. God created the sun and moon worlds at Sahasra-dal-Kanwal in the Astral Plane, which helps the souls to begin the inner journey.

During meditation, your creativity helps you become aware of what already exists. The fact is that you cannot ever imagine something which already does not exist. Your imagination is capable of creating the whole of its creation. Man is related to the inner worlds through the subconscious mind, storing most known and unknown information. All lower forms are limited in spiritual awareness and they are still going through the wheel of eighty-four.

Creation is finished; nothing is ever to be created; it is only manifested. Each soul's journey is a very long process and it goes through eighty-four hundred thousand lives. The soul is immortal, begins its long journey and enters an elemental kingdom. It passes into the mineral kingdom and then to rock imprisonment. Next, it goes to vegetable and then the tree kingdom, which is a half-awakened state, whereas the rock state was almost a whole sleep state.

Next is the animal, the bird kingdom, conscious and aware of its surroundings. After a long journey, the soul takes a human life form and realises its individuality and awareness of its creator, God. Some of our lives are very passive, whereas others are very active. Inactive lives are helpless because they cannot move from a given space or fight back, like tree life. Animal life forms are relatively active and they try to defend themselves by biting or running away.

Humans still want to hunt them for pleasure, which lands them on creating a large karma scale. This becomes the cause of their suffering, amongst other misdeeds. Man still denies any wrongdoing because he has the five passions of the mind, which misleads in believing man rules others. When you rule, others act as enslaved people. There is another lowest creation of four elements. First, are earth creatures called gnomes; they are in charge of earth elements such as gold, silver, metals and minerals.

Next are salamanders, fire elements that look like small lizards or dragons. The next element is undines; water spirits take care of sea life. The next element is the sylphs, relating to air spirits or fairies. After this long process, the soul enters human life and progresses to angels and total freedom from the lower worlds. To have any spiritual success, we must learn to love all of God's creation; without love, nothing exists.

It is love that binds you to God and it is also this love that unbinds you from evil and sets your feet on the path to righteousness. If you cannot learn to love all of its creation, you will never see the face of God or its representatives. Once you do see the face of the Lord, you will never be the same. In the higher worlds, there is pure Spirit with no religion, nothing to travel and nowhere to go; It Just Is. Lower worlds are known as a training ground for souls to take responsibility for each action taken consciously.

Once you learn this truth, you are not far from your goal. The soul of each person is inborn and indestructible. It has no age, no classification according to physical measures and beyond matter, energy, space and time. Because of this ability, the soul is the experiencer and moulds into any given life form. Two souls can occupy one body. When all other worldly things need their own space to exist visibly, at the same time, the soul is always an invisible entity.

After going through a long line of reincarnation systems, you have attained lots of God-awareness and now you want to lead a spiritual life. Questions arise within; 'Who am I? Where did I come from? Why am I here? Where am I going after death?' These questions will lead you to search for a spiritual guru and one day, you will be sitting in the presence of your creator. Once we have explored all of learning in the lower worlds, it is time to leave this world and become assistants in heaven.

Successful people learn the art of spiritual travel and are capable of breaking the silver cord, not to enter into this world again. That is, leaving this world with its free will or you may go through some sickness to clear some remaining karma. The soul can leave through a chosen spiritual chakra (pineal gland), whereas others use lower chakras. Leaving the body at the end is no more painful than birth. Accidental deaths can be painful.

Most animals face accidental deaths and are sometimes painful to watch. The soul is still within other wraps, known as mental, causal and astral bodies, to meet the king of the dead. For those who have achieved spiritual freedom, their souls leave the physical bodies and they remove astral, causal and mental bodies on their respective planes. These bodies become obsolete with no further use and they disperse naturally into nothing.

Dispersing the physical body becomes the responsibility of loved ones. Death indicates spiritual freedom and being in the presence of its creator God or returning to life on the physical plane and clearing its remaining karma. I am not connected or a follower of any religion, so I have written this on neutral ground because our God is neutral. There is only one God when religious followers say, 'This is my God and that is your God.' This leads to their failure point.

May you know yourself and your creator, God.

DWELLERS IN GOD

Those who dwell in the presence of God are the most fortunate people. This is the ultimate goal of all spiritual Seekers but only a few manage to make it this far. It is easily said but very hard to grasp and it's even hard to maintain this state of consciousness. Only a few chosen souls can manage to do this. At the same time, Spirit or God is backing them up; otherwise, it is difficult in the lower worlds.

Every spiritual Seeker wants to dwell in the worlds of God but only one person per million is successful. Many are making false statements. Following any saint for a few years or reading, spiritual literature does not make you a dweller in God. You have gained some mental knowledge and feel that you have become the knower of truth. When the truth is many miles away from you, this is the difference between knowledge and knowingness.

You can only dwell in God when you breathe, smell, eat, hear and sleep Spirit. In other words, when God has become your natural occupation of living, anything else is your second choice. These dwellers in God are faithful saints; although they are living in the physical world, their presence is always in pure spiritual worlds and waits to follow God's instructions to assist wherever possible. They are faithful assistants of Spirit. They are the knowers of truth and lead others to do the same.

As far as this world is concerned, they become very lonely but never alone; God's presence is always with them. When you know that God is with you all the time, I don't think you want to socialise with anyone. There is nothing you want to know or discuss with others. Discussion with anyone in the lower world is a waste of time. 'What do these people want to discuss with you? Most of their problems are self-created and due to that, they are suffering.

Their problems do not interest you. Every suffering or problem is karma, which must be paid in full. Dwellers in God learned this long ago. They can guide others not to create any karma and pay-back if any has been created. When any person is willing to sort out their wrong-doings and ask Spirit for guidance, it is always given. Dwellers in God are always silent and they do not enjoy the company of others because people are often searching for human company to entertain themselves.

This whole world is meeting regularly and many cannot do without meeting friends every day. Some always want a particular person not to be out of sight all day; this is mental attachment. Most of them are so busy making money or establishing their names. All these things or ideas take your mind off God and you can never be a dweller in God. Neither are those who claim to be so religious but are involved in some religious wars.

All jihadists are misled people and those who commit such acts are the victims of some altered destiny. There is so much anger within, boiling inside to come out. Their rage is beyond control but it is the wrong way of expressing it. You are going to kill someone whom you never knew or met. If people around you change the destiny of any person, then the results are catastrophic. They could have been the dwellers of God but there is something that keeps them away from it.

They are so close to God yet far, far away. When the saint becomes pure in his heart and dedicated to Spirit has cleared all his karma, he can think of nothing but Spirit. Then reality appears. It is the purity that meets reality. Light and sound overpower thoughts and you lose interest in physical activities. You still are a physical person but do not feel part of it. The feeling of music within and spiritual sensation all the time, you are dwelling in the spiritual fountain and are peaceful.

You cannot explain it to anyone but people can see it on your countenance. Once you experience this, it is good enough to last for a lifetime. Those who dwell in Spirit all the time are fortunate and become assistants of God. Humans often want to leave their homes and meet other people. They cannot sit in one place because they cannot keep their minds still. They are searching for something to satisfy themselves; there is no patience and unbearable pressure in their mind.

I hear from many friends, 'I just want to drop everything, pick up my bags and go on seaside holidays.' This is quite the opposite of the dwellers in God; going on holidays, attending musical parties and having any other celebration is very irritating. All these activities are a total waste of time and they take your mind or self from the presence of God. To the dwellers in God, all their requirements are taken care of wherever they are, although their needs are small and basic.

They always dwell in the present moment and no thoughts are given to the future. They do not pray or submit any self-petition; their faith in God is a law unto itself. Even if they don't get it, they are content with total satisfaction. The failure of most of humankind is desires. They are never satisfied with whatever they have. Although most people in this world are religious, religions are the basis of wishes and they are used as such.

The priest suggests one pray and God will meet the wishes. Priests wouldn't know what God is or how to dwell in God. Humans often suffer because they live in a self-created world full of negativity. The dwellers live in God's world, which are pure and peaceful. You simply be and enjoy; in self-created worlds, you suffer.

In search of peace, the man knocks on many religious doors. There are many ways to go in but it isn't easy to get out once entered. This is the struggle most Seekers face, this is the point when a Seeker wants to move closer to God but religion comes in the way. Religious scriptures often point to 'The Way to God,' but followers fail to read and learn the correct contents of its direction.

May you find the way in and become a dweller in God.

FAITH

Faith is total reliance on the Spirit and spiritual Master in our teachings. This is the foundation of a spiritual journey into the inner world. Without faith, although you are following the teachings, you are more or less a sceptic. You must cross the boundary of doubt to become an open channel for the Spirit. Once you experience this flow, there is no turning back. You are the sailor exploring the ocean of God, where there is no beginning or end.

Every thought or imagination turns into reality. Now you are the symbol of Spirit and people look at you as the knower of the truth. Faith on this path is not the same as religion. Their faith is based on a set of religious doctrines. By following a set of spiritual principles; they will achieve the vision of God as dictated by their clergymen. All these followers believe everything is real but it is nothing other than blind faith.

Do you know that most population of this world is living in blind faith to whatever is their concern? The setback of these people is that they do not have the guts to question their respective leaders. 'What is your practical success in our religion? Instead of giving a direct answer, you will hear several religious verses from their holy books written by their religious founder. These prophets left this world a long time and their scholars have written many holy books or at least updated them.

This is the case for almost all religions. Ordinary people have some problems in their lives and due to many fears, they respect their leaders and believe what they're told. Regarding these knowers of truth, if you ask them not to use your religion or the experience of your holy man, tell us what you know about God. They will be dumbstruck and lost for words because they never thought of God from that angle. This will act as a hammer on their heads and an awakening point in Spirit.

If they catch this point sincerely, they will never utter a single word to indicate this is 'my' or 'your' religion. All religious people have faith in their respective following but unfortunately, it is not leading them anywhere other than for or against other religions. Most of the wars are religious-based. Each person carries a spiritual spark within, known as the soul. Ill thinking or killing another person is against the will of God but the people who kill in the name of God feel proud and call themselves martyrs.

This is a clear indication that all religions are man-made to suit their needs or the circumstances. Any religious scripture written by a prophet leads the individual or soul to God. The clergy fails to convey a proper message to the followers or they modify the actual text according to their limited knowledge or to suit the demands of followers. Wrong interpretation of actual text sometimes becomes a barrier between God and soul.

God created all the universes for souls to experience their spiritual journeys. These misled faiths have created a whirlpool where there is no way out once you enter. Once in a while, some souls find their way out; even then, they need the guts to quit their following. Once you do manage to leave any religious teaching, the beliefs you followed for years will still have a pull on you until your last breath in this world.

To be pure of religious thoughts, you need a solid foundation and a spiritual teacher who can create universal thought within yourself. Universal thought is the beginning of any live experience. Once your journey begins into the inner worlds and you receive spiritual revelation or pearls of wisdom, your faith in the Spirit will strengthen. Now you become the knower of truth. You don't need to follow any religious doctrine.

The answer to your questions will be at hand and the more you tune in to Spirit, the more you will know. Your faith in Spirit is such that all your questions or problems will cease. Now you understand the system of God. God has created every person and situation for a purpose. All you have to do is to sail the oceans with ease. For any religious person, it does not matter how he prays. God hardly listens but some problems resolve themselves with time or other means.

The credit goes to one's religion or guru. 'Why does God not listen to them? Because their questions or problems are biased towards themselves. Hardly any religion teaches the purpose of universal thought because they know once their followers have a universal opinion, the beliefs will lose their grip on them. Any person with a universal view is always a free entity, understands the meaning of free will and will also allow others to be themselves.

Some religions claim to bring heaven on earth and universal thought is the way. This religion claims to bring heaven on earth; in their minds, it is well-established that 'this is mine and yours.' One day, Jehovah's witness believers knocked on my door and persisted that I should read their monthly magazine because they wanted to bring peace on earth. As long as I was listening, they were happy.

Once I told them that I had written a book about God and offered it very politely, they disappeared into thin air. It would help if you practiced what you preach. Their primary purpose is to convert people to join them. All religions have very loyal members. The more loyal you are, the more religious you feel. Some religions ask their loyal members to donate ten percent of their earnings. My question is, 'To promote what? The more you promote religious thought, the more ethical followers should be.

Most of them are but still, it does not lead them to universal thought or individuality. God created each soul as an individual. 'Do you know even twins are not alike? You will find some differences in looks and ideas. Loyalty to any religion teaches the individual to lead a good, honest life but it does not prepare or guarantee one's place in heaven or indicate the time of one leaving this world. According to your religious doctrine, the faith will weaken if things don't appear or materialise.

Broken or shakeable faith can create catastrophic situations in your life and you could be out of balance for life. The origin of new teachings or religion is always based on broken faith; the religion you followed was not as you expected. Most religions spring out of another religion; Sikhism out of Hinduism, Christianity out of Judaism. Faith without any spiritual experience is not worth it; it holds no value without proof.

Despite no experience, millions of followers will keep their faith alive because their ancestors said so. At present, we live in a civilised world with high education standards and can understand religious thought or practice for its clarity and blind faith leads you nowhere. God sends its messengers or prophets time after time to lead the souls back to God's world. They only serve the purpose of teaching or showing the way to be in the presence of God.

Once you learn this, there is no mediator between God and the soul. It is the individual journey of the soul. Once you have faith in Spirit or God and are unwaveringly loyal, I have no words to describe your spiritual gain. Many fortunate people manage to find a true guru who can lead souls back to their inner worlds. During this union of Master and Seeker, many miracles take place. This will build up your faith more-strong.

But at the same time, these miracles can divert you from your true seeking or original spiritual goal. Faith alone is not good enough; seeking within during meditation is crucial. Once you become the knower of truth or reality, do you know this word **faith** also disappears now you are part of Spirit? Your life will go along with the flow of Spirit. You will take any experience in life as the will of God.

You are so strong that no chains of this world can hold you to this physical ground. You fly like an eagle in the sky and you are a hawk who is watchful for all your karma, action and reactions. Your success will lead others to have unshakeable faith and one day; they will be the sailors of the oceans of God and lead millions to do the same. Now you know it is the faith within and your teacher; nothing is impossible. There is nothing you cannot do or understand.

You are not here to pass the time but you are born to lead this world. Your faith will be tested many times during your spiritual journey by your teacher. Never feel discouraged. The Master is always standing next to you to ensure that you never fail. God did not create any soul who is a failure. You are so dear to God because you are part of it. It will make sure that you return to God as an assistant. The more knowingness you have, the more responsibility it will give you. One day you will return as a prophet of God.

A new born child has natural faith in its mother's arms; everything is provided without fail and it has a smiling face. We struggle in life because we try to do things our way. Have faith in God and you will receive all without fail.

FIRST CAUSE

The origin of everything is God. God is the first cause and it created the spiritual planes and respective rulers. All the higher worlds are still part of this first cause; there is nothing equal or opposite, day or night. These higher planes operate very much as God does, in pure Spirit. As we move below the dividing line or soul plane, that is where the first cause turns into effect and every action reacts.

This is when the battle between negative and positive begins. Whatever you see in this world is a reaction to or effect of this first cause because God is the creator. In Christianity, it is expressed through the story of Adam and Eve. They were placed naked by God in the Garden of Eden amongst all animals to live peacefully and God advised them that they could eat any fruit from any tree except the tree of knowledge.

This tree of knowledge was the key to crossing over the wall to see what lies on the other side. It is believed the serpent tempted Adam and Eve to eat this fruit. The serpent is a symbol of a negative spirit. As soon as Adam and Eve ate this fruit, that acted as key to the awareness of negative power and they began to think. Before, their minds were acting as spiritual minds. As soon as this happened, they became aware of their nakedness and all other negative powers or thoughts began to rise.

They began to know who was human and who was animal. Self-protection is required from the animal kingdom, it was not the animals who wanted to attack them but it was the fear within and in their eyes. Animals only attack when they see the picture of fear in your eyes. Our belief in this theory of karma is different; we believe that the lord of karma attached some karma to each soul to begin its journey into the lower planes. By eating that fruit, Adam and Eve committed karma or as Christians believe, the original sin.

All our sufferings are based on this original sin. Sexuality, fear, attachment and all other passions came with original sin. According to Christian texts, Adam and Eve were here 6,022 years ago or around 4004 BC, when Hindu written text is approximately ten thousand years old. I think Christian scholars need to make some corrections here. I only said according to information provided on the Internet.

Negative power can blind any person to committing any kind of karma and now we are so deeply involved in the world or the cycle of Kali-Yuga that we have forgotten about the first cause. That is why the question arises, 'Where is God? Has anyone seen God? Every person has created a fort around oneself. Anyone outside this fort is taken as an enemy. You will have a few near or dear ones and any other is not accepted on many grounds such as religion, colour and country.

God is the first cause within each soul as a little spark. This is our link from soul to soul and from each soul to God. Due to negativity within or around, you fail to see that person standing next to you is part of God and, at the same time, part of yourself. 'Why did you fail to recognise this spark in the person standing next to you? Because it is not your fault altogether.

Due to negativity within that person, he also failed to express this spark. You can see his actions and deceiving eyes and you do not trust him. We have forgotten the first cause but have become the agents of Kal and the veil of illusion covers everything. We always complain of our suffering. 'Why do we suffer? If we are suffering, then why are we complaining? Because we have forgotten our original sin or karma, which we committed and now it is repayment time. When we fail to pay back, that is our negative quality.

The suffering begins through physical problems or ailments and we cannot bear this pain. There is a cause within cause and effect within effect. Every person or soul is a circle itself which covers the whole eternity. God is the original cause and the large circle and we are within God's circle. At the same time, God is also within your small circle. This is the riddle that is so easy to understand and at the same time, it's complicated too.

FUTURE FORECASTS

This is the favourite subject of many people but I have been avoiding it for many years. I haven't written about it because once people come to know that you have said something, their curiosity compels them to find out more about it. I always tried not to get involved in this kind of discussion. Over the years, I saw so many visions of future happenings but I lost their contents because I did not write them in my diary. Now I will briefly write what I can recall and make notes in the future.

Helicopters

I mentioned this to so many friends or people in my circle back in 1990. Most car travelling will turn into mini helicopters approximately fifty years from now. Due to future congestion, cars will fly in the air and travel routes will be designed. New drivers will pass their car tests accordingly. We can use several routes and each vehicle will be classed as to what route it can use. By 2040 or early, you will begin to see this in practice.

Future Destruction

I saw this vision on 9 November 1994. Extensive destruction will occur in this world approximately thirty-five years from now. It will be around the year 2029/30 unless the vibrations of this world change. At present, all governments are very aggressive toward gaining power. I hope they can write some kind of mutual peaceful treaty.

New Earth Planet

Most religions mention the end of this world. At present, that is far, far away. As I said, big destruction will take place around 2029/30. That will not be the end of this world but a big shake-up. After that, people will come to some positive realisation. The end of this world is approximately 400,000 years away from now. Once this happens, Spirit will shift the remaining souls to a new planet. Not as mentioned by many religions that this earth will stay in darkness for the years of Maha-Yuga.

Then God will sprinkle Spirit and this world will change into a new world as it was initially. Maha-Yuga is the combined years of four ages; golden, silver, bronze and iron. I made this forecast back in 2012 to my friends that the new earth planet will be found soon and that it is going to be our future planet. I was pleased when I learned that a new planet was discovered by NASA on 22 February 2017. It is three times the size of our planet earth. There are several other planets yet to be found.

Weather Changes

Currently, we use coal, gas or electricity to warm our houses during cold weather. This is going to change. We have almost run out of coal and soon we will run out of gas, petrol and diesel. At the same time, we will try not to use them because of global warming. Nature has provided us with sun rays and water to meet most of our needs when used with new technology. Windows of our houses will take complete transformation. They will provide and control the desired temperature within the home. At the same time, new glass will also act as curtains, controlled by the sun's light or with remote controls.

Future Housing

Skyscrapers have great architectural designs to be admired; however, this is going to change. It is going to be hazardous living at these heights. Global warming and carbon monoxide pollution will rise, which will lead to many health problems. During the first and second world wars, underground nuclear shelters were made to protect us. In the future, new houses will be built low or under the surface. This will be considered healthy living because it is scientifically proven that most gases travel upwards. Heavy gases similar to LPG or any others will be discontinued. An underground living will be the pride of the future.

Population

The population of this world is increasing; however, in the next five hundred years, it will show signs of a decrease. It will be the biggest worry for the whole world in one thousand years. People will begin to love each other and try to save whomever they can. Kal is getting stronger by the day but common sense will prevail later.

Death

Death will be conquered in the future. Science is making progressive strides in exploring other universes and religions fail followers to show God's world, as mentioned in religious writings. Religions fail to produce faithful saints who can teach spiritual travel. Religions have become more or less materialistic and political. There will be independent saints who will teach spiritual travel and our scientists will break the speed of light.

With this combined effort, people will be able to use both means to travel to other universes. At present, everyone fears death but people will be able to visit these places while still living in the future. Death will become the right of all people; either you want to live or die. Once this future travelling becomes a natural phenomenon, people will prefer to live in other worlds. Voluntary death and astral migration to upper regions will become tomorrow's world.

Most Third World countries want to migrate to Europe, Australia or America. People will prefer to have relations on the Astral Plane or any other in the future. As the chaos in this world increases, people will find there is no future living in this world.

Future Lie Detector

At present Narco test is carried out to find the truth behind serious crimes committed by suspects. This person under trial is injected with Sodium Pentothal or Sodium Amytal, commonly known as 'Truth Sermns.' These drugs put the suspect into a semi-conscious state. So, during questioning, the required information can be obtained.

The second test is the Lie detector test based on polygraphs. When questions are asked from the individual, it monitors the; Blood pressure, Pulse rate, Respiration and Skin conductivity to get results. These results are 95% accurate.

However, this test has been deceived by a very calm individual.

Both tests will be obsolete and replaced by new vision test cameras in the future. It will reveal the results as seen in the 'Eyes.' So far, we have overlooked that there are two main culprits behind every crime or deception. It is your mind and two eyes. What you see instantly is in your mind or vice versa. During questioning, any suspect can tell lies but eyes express what is going on within your mind.

GOD-REALISATION

This is one of the simplest ways to explain what is Self and God-realisation, using these diagrams. For example, a drop of water (soul) is trapped inside this plastic dummy (physical body). It cannot get out unless someone can open it. This can only open if we have the spiritual Master to guide us and with his help, we manage to balance our five passions of the mind. We know our lower bodies and understand their function during our journey into the lower worlds.

With the help of the Master, we have explored most of these lower spiritual planes. At present, we are on the verge of realising ourselves as souls. Once we find this opening and manage to travel internally or externally on our own, we can know our true identity is the soul, not the physical body, as we have understood for years. This is the first step of realisation. There is a lot more to know and understand. At this point, we should live our lives as directed by God or Spirit.

Drop of water as Soul

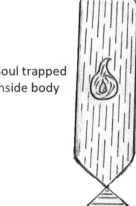

Soul trapped
inside body

Now we have found the opening
Soul is free to explore.

Glass of water as symbol of God
Ocean of love and Mercy.
Now becomes part of Ocean.

It depends on your effort and how long or to what extent you can live your life as directed by God. That will lead you to have God-realisation in this life. Once you are in a God-realised state, it depends on how long you can dwell in this state of consciousness. It is a big responsibility to maintain this state of consciousness; otherwise, you could be Self-realised only. The higher you go, the easier it is to drop from your position.

May success be yours.

GOD'S EMPIRE

All religions claim their empire or the number of memberships they have, how dominating they are or their growth throughout this world. They have very clever ideas to spread their message. Some religions are losing members because they have failed to accommodate the expectations of their followers. The whole of creation, known as souls, are part of God. Due to spiritual links, they cannot be separated from God.

The total number is very similar to our bank accounts. For example, I have five different bank accounts and place different amounts of money according to my needs. One account holds £6000, another has £5000 and the rest three hold £1000. The total is £12000. As long as my original total remains safe and sound, it should not bother me mentally which account has more or less.

It is the same with God. As long as all souls learn from their experiences in the lower worlds, it does not bother God because all the lessons cannot be learned in one religion or system. Those religions claiming large membership are proud of their religious leaders but to God, its children are playing with toys. 'Which child has more toys than the other? Does it matter to God? No, because God knows that they are all his upon counting at the end of the day.

This is the point all religions fail to understand. They are fighting with each other while not understanding who is the boss and owns every soul. To any religious body, they are their followers. One day they will know and understand. In this discourse, I will try to explain the whole structure of God very briefly. There is an infinite void beyond human measurements and this void is full of silence. In the centre is God.

God is formless and beyond any known limits. God does not take any form because it is part of creation. Its creation has 8,400,000 facets and on this basis, it is part of every single face. At the same time, it has none because it is within each soul; no one can claim God looks like them. God has kept itself on a neutral basis. Similarly, we can see or experience our mirrored image of God once we reach any understanding of it, known as spiritual awareness.

All religions know God by many names. The names are used according to their experience or how close they have managed to be in God's presence. God, Allah, Hari and Prabhu are the names or suggested by the founders of each religion and their followers believe these are the actual names of God. To God, it does not matter how you contact it. Learning spiritual experience in the lower worlds is essential.

Light and Sound

Communication of God to its creation throughout the universes is based on twin pillars, divine light and sound. Light is knowledge and provides illumination; otherwise, all creations would have been here but visibility to each other would have been none. Sound is the bonding part of putting all the particles together and in different arrangements. A combination of both is known as Spirit, which sustains the entire creation.

Awakened souls can feel the presence of Spirit and more awakened ones can feel the presence of God too. Awakened souls can also see the light in many shades and hear the sound in many melodies. Light is a pure brilliant white shade but as it travels from God through the higher planes and then proceeds into the lower planes, its shade or colour changes according to the vibrations; pure white, light golden, golden, purple, blue orange, pink and green.

Sound also changes its melody as it passes from higher to lower worlds; silence, whirlpool, woodwinds, a thousand violins, a humming sound, wind, flute, buzzing bees, running water, tinkling brass bells, the roar of the sea and thunder. Light and sound as Spirit is invested in each soul to keep this communication alive so that all souls can feel the presence of God. It also knows the well-being of each soul.

Sound is continuously rolling within each soul; this is the lifeline of each soul. Sound flows from God's world to the lower worlds and travels back to its source. This flow is known as centre petal and fugal. These are the sound waves for each soul to travel back and forward to its creator. Sound acts as a vehicle and light act as knowledge or a torch to see the spiritual path. The number of these waves is infinite to accommodate the whole creation.

Nine Pillars of God

I don't think religions know what I will say, apart from one or two paths. I call them the 'Nine Super Souls.' God

81

especially created them to assist in developing all higher planes and keep maintenance of all spiritual planes, universes and Planets. Super souls are only answerable to God itself and repair any unbalance created by negative vibrations.

If these Masters are not here, it will not take long to explode stars, the sun's heat will be unbearable and the outcome will be disastrous. Many of the disasters are due to this unbalance or are created by nature to maintain its balance. Nine Super Souls do not communicate with any person or being and they move along silently to do their spiritual endeavour as required or advised by God.

God's World

God's world is created to accommodate many other required facilities. Anami-Lok and its lord are responsible for creating new souls. At the same time, this is the only plane where souls are purified for a special purpose. Although all souls are pure as part of God, when the new living Master of the time is given the responsibility, his soul is taken back to its original creation point to do clean up of any impurities. Due to the clean-up or creation of souls, it is called the ocean of love and mercy.

As for Agam-Lok, if any soul manages to come this far due to its spiritual unfoldment, the soul becomes aware of its creator, known as God-realisation. The soul knows, 'I am not only a soul but am part of God.' Very few saints have managed to come this far. Golden temples in the Alakh, Alaya and Hakikat planes provide spiritual education for the soul to have God-realisation. All these planes have their respective lords. I cannot think of any appropriate words to express their beingness.

Satnam Ji

Any of the above lords cannot be seen by any soul to communicate. When required, they purposely manifest for the experience of any soul when taken by the Master of the time; otherwise, these beings remain invisible. After creating all, any soul is housed in the soul plane. Souls on this plane are visible to each other for relevant communication. Although God is neutral and formless, this is the requirement to create a link between souls and God. God manifested itself as its first personification, known as Satnam Ji.

This is why in Sikhism, it is known as Akal-Murat. Akal is the opposite to Kal or negative power and therefore, Akal means formless and Murat means a replica. Satnam Ji is the replica of God for any soul to be seen or communicate with. Upon this meeting of soul and Satnam Ji, the silent voice within feels, 'I am He and He is me.' Materialistically speaking, the soul plane is the storehouse for all souls. Satnam Ji becomes the keeper of all souls and records each soul's journey from the beginning till it becomes God-realised.

Guru Nanak of Sikhism; is called Satnam Ji the Karta-Purakh, which means responsible for all souls. God gave Satnam Ji the responsibility for all souls and for being seen when this communication is required. As the replica of God, a soul is neutral and has its being in the purely spiritual planes. There was not much learning for souls. Anami is the creator and Satnam Ji is the caretaker of souls.

Vairaagy Masters

These Masters play a very crucial role in God's empire. 'You may wonder who they are? There is no such time when God does not have one representing its message in God's kingdom. This is a chain or unbroken line of Masters, with all those Masters who have done their duties in the lower worlds and are gone beyond but a few selective ones remain behind to assist God, present living Master, Nine Super Souls or the lord of planes.

God

God created the lower planes and trinity lords to look after the creation. It is pure Spirit in higher worlds but divided into negative and positive in the lower worlds. All the lower worlds are based on duality. At any time, no one can claim, 'I am as pure as God,' while residing in the worlds of Kal. Kal is a name given to the spiritual power to provide schooling for each soul.

Multiple tasks were created by Kal's power for souls to pass through so that they can learn lessons to become assistants of God. According to the number of lower planes; further embodiments are given to each soul as garments to wear so a soul can express itself on each plane. Mental, Causal, Astral and Physical are planes and these layers or bodies cover each soul. Our spiritual experience will eliminate each layer until it sheds all layers into a pure or neutral soul.

This is why we use the word unfoldment. The soul was folded within these layers to be unfolded. The lower worlds are vast in size and have several lords or keepers but a new trinity was created to care for souls' welfare in the lower worlds. All religions have different names but they are known as Brahma, Vishnu and Shiva in Hinduism.

Trinity Gods

Brahma is the creator of lower bodies. Vishnu is known as the preserver and his responsibility is to provide food or shelter. Shiva Ji is the destroyer, so every lower body must be destroyed after its allotted time. In the lower worlds, nothing is permanent. Whatever body, man, animal, a tree is given limited time before it ends one spiritual experience and begins a new life. This system is called the wheel of eighty-four and each soul has to incarnate time after time for several lives to mature and become an assistant of God.

Shakti

Female energy is worshipped around the world by many different names. It is considered the mother of this world. Hinduism centres around the incarnation of feminine power, known as Kali Mata; she worships like Brahma, Vishnu and Shiva. The importance of the Mother Goddess is that Brahma creates but for birthing a child, one needs a womb. Vishnu is the preserver but the child needs someone to feed him. This is why and how the female energy helps create God's empire.

Maze

These lords created a maze for our schooling to help us learn and get purified. Many attachments are given, so we are busy with five passions of the mind. This is the puzzle and the soul has to find a way to become free once more. So negative or Kal provide the chain and spiritual Master is here to free the soul or show the way of getting free.

Karma

As soon as any soul leaves the soul plane and goes into the lower worlds for schooling, karma is attached to it to monitor the soul's progress. The soul is covered by the other four bodies; mental, causal, astral and physical. On the physical plane, the physical body represents the soul to each other.

Lower worlds are impermanent, but illusion and the five passions are so strong that most people have forgotten they are souls. They believe that the mind and physical bodies are the leading players in the lower worlds for survival. This is the reason people suffer.

Suffering

Suffering means going through some experience, either positive or negative. Suffering means the soul has learned some lesson or become aware of some spiritual point, known as awareness. The soul is the knower of truth, part of God itself but it must explore every issue or situation. The five passions are there to incarnate desires within and each desire will lead the soul to learn another lesson. Kal creates the situation for the soul to pass through every lesson with distinction.

Most religions teach that negative power is bad. This is the statement given by frail people or religions. Every single lesson is a step forward and towards the Creator. We live our lives emotionally based, with attachment to our relations. Our weaknesses push us towards God for any mercy. Why are we looking for this mercy from God or any saint? Because we cannot bear the pain of our suffering or what we have created.

During our incarnations and dealing with other souls, we overlooked or did not pay back what we borrowed from others; it could be food, money, property or physical care. What is suffering; it is the karma we are going through, where someone else is in the commanding position and we are weak or with less authority. This suffering could be in the shape of mental or physical torture but we have forgotten that we put this person in a similar situation.

In the lower world, no one is doing any favour to anyone or we are not suffering without any reason. It is the theory of action and reaction, equal and opposite, cause and effect and yin and yang. We are always happy and enjoy receiving gifts but often we feel irritated when repayments are demanded. It is only exchanging karma and it is always recommended to create good karma, which means learning to give instead of receive.

Spiritual Master

Negative power creates situations according to our karma. The spiritual Master shows us how to go through situations with ease. The spiritual Master is the key player in God's empire, He is everywhere, from God to the physical plane and all souls of any plane can communicate with him for assistance. His authority is consented to by God. He is not head of any religion or chosen by the public, whether religious or politically based.

His birth is planned by Satnam Ji and the lord of karma from where he will be able to give the message of God. He is from the unbroken line of Masters since the Golden-Age and it will continue till the end of Kali-Yuga (Iron-Age). This line of Masters will not remain for too long in one country. It'll be no more than one or two Masters and then it must shift its spiritual centre to another country, where the presence of this Master is needed.

If this seat of spiritual power remains in one country for too long, then it will not take long for pure individual teachings to turn into a new religion. His purpose in life is to lead souls back to Satnam Ji. That is why he is not a reformer, as most saviours claim. Reformers bring change to some parts of this world. God has created the system for the benefit of souls' learning. Reformers deceive this purpose. God can bring change to any system in a split second.

Religious followers or leaders are happy with reformers because they try to make life easier and all are temporary. Reformers are sympathetic with humans, which is the quality of Kal or lower worlds. God operates beyond duality on a neutral basis. The Hindu saviour Krishna came and brought the change. Napoleon, Alexander the Great and lately Hitler have tried to bring change according to their thinking.

Any change which is not in line with the planning of the lord of karma upsets the system and alters the purpose or destiny of souls. All these killings done in religion or politics serve no purpose but to delay the soul's journey. Holy wars have been fought in all religions for thousands of years. We are still the same people, moaning, groaning and fighting. This will carry on forever as long as we are in the lower worlds. Reforming the system is a temporary solution.

God does not give authority to any person, religious leader, saviour or reformer to take the life of another human or any of its creation. Truth often hurts. Any saviour who holds a weapon to kill another creature or tries to show authority in this manner violates spiritual law. God does not kill or destroy any soul whatsoever. 'Then who are we to do this? All these religious saviours are our heroes but they are tiny players in this empire of God.

We should try to lead any person; we believe is wrong-doing to do good karma. Ending his life does not serve a purpose. In his next life, he might do worse. Any person who wants to leave this world must become universal in thought. He may be born in any religion but he must accept all creation as part of himself. Be yourself and let the others be. If you cannot do this, you have created a wall between yourself and God and you will never be a key player in God's empire.

These living Masters are beyond religion and will remain that way. He is not the heritage of any religion or country. He usually is shy and not known by many. By the time people find out about him, he is already gone from that arena.

LORD OF KARMA

Karma is attached upon leaving the soul plane and spiritual progress is based on this. Every incarnation will teach the soul from a different dimension and we have to go through millions of tasks. The lord of karma places the soul at certain places through birth, which gives the soul the best learning opportunity.

We often take this learning as suffering. At the end of the soul's present physical life span, the lord of karma sends the angels to bring back the soul in its presence and records the learning in the register. Depending on what you have not learned yet, he will place you somewhere on the physical plane for your next task.

Heaven and Hell

There are sections in his place where each soul is kept until he prepares a suitable place for the next lesson. Religions often call this place heaven and hell. Priests tell many dramatic or scary stories to scare people. They tell these stories because I can guarantee you they have never seen the places themselves. Each soul is very precious to God, being part of itself and each soul is sent into the lower worlds to gain spiritual experience to become the assistant of God.

We send our children to school for learning and they do many wrong things. 'Do we hang them upside down to punish them or boil them in hot water or oil? No. We try to show them how not to repeat the same mistake. The lord of karma does the same. Instead of punishing us, he sends us down again in this world till we execute that learning and pass with distinction. The lord of karma creates the situations for our learning; this is why all these lower worlds are called training grounds for souls.

This is God's empire to create souls and bring them into the lower worlds. The lords in each plane help the soul to learn further. In some future discourse, we will discuss many spiritual bases to control and keep the balance of all universes. They are the way stations communicate with higher planes for the landing of UFOs. Spiritual scriptures provide knowledge for souls ready to work with the spiritual Master of the time. He will lead each soul through a journey to golden temples and eventually, he will lead the soul to its true home, the soul plane and above.

Non-believers

In the modern scientific world, you will find non-believers in God. 'Why don't they believe? They have many reasons because, somehow, they do not feel the presence of God in this world. It is not God who failed them; their birth religion was unable to express God's presence. They always talk about their guru, who God sent to convey its message. This guru was here for a few years but now he is gone and his religion has become an inactive religion because the flow of Spirit is not there as it used to be.

Followers believe the Master is still around but the new caretakers (priests) don't know what to do. They create a system that is less of religion and more of politics. Some sincere Seekers do not feel the presence of God as they believed to be in their religion and lose faith and walk away from it, saying, 'I don't believe God exists.' You will often notice these non-believers or sceptic people become faithful followers of God. They are waiting for a spiritual spark to be seen somewhere and live again.

The living Master is here if anyone wants to experience God or its empire in this life. There are so many yoga systems that practice the Kundalini. If anyone wants to experience psychic powers known as illusion, you can follow this route. God has provided the answer to every question; it is up to you to know or ignore the answers. That is your free will. But never say God does not exist.

GOING BEYOND PHYSICAL

All the lower worlds are subject to duality and they have a few suns according to the light required because they are more luminous than the physical world. All higher planes have flat surfaces. They are beyond time or duality; they do not have to orbit to acquire any illumination. Souls do not sleep as part of God; they are always in the arms of the Spirit. This is a small riddle that most religious people do not grasp.

Most religions will never know what higher planes are because they are all stuck in heaven and hell. Their discussion always revolves around these two words. This universe is so vast that to travel physically takes a long time. Can you imagine if you have to travel all the lower worlds and the worlds beyond, 'How long would it take? This is one way of travelling; our creator has made our journey simple.

It is very similar to our present computer science. God made attachments or folders full of details of all universes or planes ever created. All you have to do is open these files and the totality is shining or opened up within yourself and precisely on the spot where you are sitting. The key to opening these files is your soul. There is no space in pure spiritual planes; nothing exists because each soul lives within the other.

There is no time or space to travel; you mock up the point to be present at and the soul will shift or find itself present here. God itself occupies this total space or void and you are part of it, so consciously, you are everywhere. Upon leaving, you will find the Astral Plane is better than our physical plane and its laws, as it is supposed to be because the presence of the king of the dead. This judge's court is always open because there is no such time when souls do not leave the physical plane.

There is no waiting time for anyone; your earned deeds must be justified then. How you can pay off outstanding karma is decided between the court king and the soul. Heavy karma often drags the soul back to the physical. Although there are two sections known as heaven and hell, you are placed according to your remaining karma. It is similar to our railway tickets when travelling first or second class. As mentioned by the priests, there are no horrible places to create fear within its followers.

Heaven means your karma is not that heavy; you may remain in this part of the Astral Plane to work out your remaining karma and progress to the next heaven, known as the causal plane. Hell means you stay there till a place of birth is prepared for you. God sent souls into the lower worlds for schooling so they could assist in its cause later. A description of hell clearly shows the depth of knowledge of any religion. The soul is not a waste; it is part of God itself.

Therefore, it is very dear to God and is cared for while waiting for the next incarnation. If you travel with the spiritual Master, that is very healthy. Otherwise, there are good souls on the Astral Plane who assist and lead you to your earned place or group of known people, such as relatives. The soul represents the astral form; similarly, it describes itself on the physical plane in a physical body.

Religions or priests always discuss heaven and hell on the Astral Plane concerning people leaving the physical. This is all they know or have read in their religious scriptures; it is all book knowledge. 'What happens to those souls progressing from astral to causal or mental? Similarly, each plane has its lord of karma and decides the fate of each soul. When a soul reaches the soul plane, it is beyond karma and comes directly under Satnam Ji's supervision.

The soul is karma-less, so it does not have to return to the lower worlds because it has attained spiritual freedom. Achieving spiritual freedom is very simple or it could be tricky depending on how you approach this experience. Your spiritual Master will guide you to follow some instructions. The base of your success depends on how successful you are in doing your spiritual exercises. Very briefly, prepare yourself for spiritual practice. Sit down in tailor fashion in a quiet room.

Keep your back erect and chin slightly up, so your Crown-Chakra, the third-eye and spine are in line. This helps Spirit enter through the Crown-Chakra easily and reach all other spiritual openings. That stirs the vibrations when reciting your spiritual word. Imagination will play a significant part in achieving your goal. Your vibrations will stir up, we have a warm feeling within our forehead and our bodies feel a slight vibrating sensation. If we can hold on to our nerve, the soul will leave through the tenth door in no time.

You will find yourself in the sub-planes of the astral plane. You will see the sun and moon world, then the lighting world zone (Ashta-Dal-Kanwal). This is the place where the spiritual Master is waiting for you. The Master will meet you in his radiant form and that will change the course of your future life because you are not the same person. You can consider yourself a spiritual traveller as well. Sahasra-Dal-Kanwal is the capital of the Astral Plane.

GOLDEN AURA & BLACK MAGIC

The spiritual force protects those following the living Master with complete sincerity. Your spiritual word is on constant recitation at the inner; then Spirit provides a spiritual shield. Wherever you go, you are within this shield. It does not matter how hard someone tries to harm you; it will not work. You will find many people around you who are not happy. They live under the influence of anger, one of the five passions of the mind.

Sometimes this anger alone does not satisfy them, so they go several steps forward and seek psychic help. This is to make sure that you are hurt in some way. This is a very pleasing experience for them. Most of the time, you will find they claim to be very religious people but they do not apply any spiritual principles in life. Anger has crowded their mentality. 'What happens when they send anger or black magic towards this true spiritual Seeker?

The Seeker is always within this invisible golden or white light. Anything sent towards him bounces back to the sender. Once this burst of anger energy or black magic cannot penetrate the spiritual shield, it generally returns to the sender, who is injured by his act. This spiritual shield is a law unto itself and it has the power to return whatever is coming towards it to the sender. This holy person is not responsible for whatever happens to the sender.

In this situation, the holy person is not a cause or effect. This sender or angry person is the cause of this situation and the impact of his own doing. You shall reap what you sow, as the saying goes. If you are following the teaching of the present Master, then Spirit acts like a mother hen who spreads her wings over her chicks to cover them when an eagle or hawk hovers over them. Little chicks have complete faith in the mother hen for protection and we should trust the inner Spirit.

Once we are tuned in to Spirit, we live peaceful and happy lives. 'Did you ever see the baby struggle in its mother's arms? The answer is no. We only suffer or struggle in life when we are scared and move away from the wings provided by the Spirit.

Trust Spirit because nothing can touch you.

GOLDEN HOUR

The golden hour does not often happen in our lives. It is a rare moment and we often miss the opportunity to enjoy it, thinking there is plenty of time. It is the moment when you could be sitting in a bliss state. I know the time when you were sitting in a bliss state and this is the time when most people are afraid. I am talking about the time before your birth in this world. This scary place is called heaven or hell in our terminology.

After the experience of death, now you are in the house of the lord of karma. Your karma is judged and now you are waiting for the next suitable family. You will find an eligible family where your karma matched the most. Still, there is no opportunity for any birth because there is no married couple in that family who could bear a child.

It may take several years before anyone could get married in that family to welcome your arrival. In this situation, you are waiting in the home provided by the lord of karma. It is a care-free period and you have been cared for by the lord of karma. I call this your golden hour. The next stage of the golden hour takes place at your birth. The child is always welcome in the family. You bring joy to the parents and family.

The love you receive is in abundance; cuddles and kisses all day, you are well fed and your smile brings joy to all around you. It is a golden hour for your parents because their wish has come true. You have nothing else to do apart from eating, sleeping and smiling. You are so happy. Do you know why? Because you don't even know about your birth. Sometimes you may not feel well or have some pain. You do acknowledge the pain but have no fear as elders do.

Do you know that you do not even acknowledge if you die when young because you don't understand what death is? You only acknowledge death once you become aware of yourself in this world. In the early days or years, you enjoy playing with toys. As long as you are playing with toys, you still have not established yourself in this world. During early death, your parents will cry because you left a deep scar in their lives.

The love you have given and the company they enjoyed is a sorrow to them, but it has been a golden hour for you. You never knew what death or fear is? This awareness of birth may take three to four years or up to seven years. Once you are aware that you are part of this world and know what pain is, your life experience becomes painful. You feel your pain and others' too and then your golden hour fades away as the responsibilities of life increase.

It could be painful as you enter the teen years if your parents have separated or your background is poor. But to some, the golden hour continues through these years. Your family needs, education or playing sports are all placed in a golden hour for you to enjoy. At present, the golden hour depends on your background. At this age, you are fully aware of yourself. Man's suffering results from his own doing; we often become careless of our surroundings.

The more you love God's creation, the more God will give you an abundance of love. If you don't care about its creation and become violent, then it is not God who does not care but your doings you have to face. With time, your golden hour seems to fade away and many sorrows surround you. Now you are married and your responsibilities increase, including providing for your children.

With time, your golden hour fades away like an old dream that once you dreamed and now it only appears as a shadow in your memory. Now it is time to experience the hour of love if you are fortunate enough. Or it could be an hour of total darkness. It is a big void and the golden hour seems far, far away, similar to fairy-tale stories. At old age, physical pain increases and the people you love may disappear. This is the experience of life you never knew before, yet many more situations are to come and teach the truth of life.

Life has taught you how to love and now it is time to learn detachment. You have to learn the art of living and once you become the master of life, it is time to leave. Your loved ones can see that you are almost ready to die. They cry and pray for your safe journey. They hold your hand, feel nothing or you can hardly hear what they say. It is your last hour and you are looking at them. They are looking at you and wondering why because you are there but are dwelling in the high.

As the body becomes numb, you feel no pain. You are waiting for the moment to leave. Angels have arrived and you are pointing the finger at them. They smile to accompany you. You can hear the lord of karma doing your accounts; if any disturbances or cries interfere, you tell everyone to be silent. That moment of crossing is most important to you. You point at any closed door for your loved ones to open with a cute smile on your face. Your last breath has stopped.

People around you begin to cry but your golden hour has just begun. You follow the same landscapes of the Astral Plane, the greenery, flowers, hills and paths you walked not long ago. They all seemed familiar because you were there only a few days ago, although it had been many physical years. You feel fresh because some kind of burden has been taken off. You are back in bliss and the lord of karma is taking care of you until your next assignment.

There are millions of people sitting in the golden hour when billions of you are afraid of going there. It is your golden hour. 'For how long? That is the will of God. I have learned a lot and there is a lot more to come. Until then, let me enjoy my golden hour. You can enjoy this blissful state or a golden hour by learning the art of dying daily, known as spiritual travel within. I have learned this long ago and it is the most peaceful moment, continuous is-ness, which is never-ending unless someone comes and disturbs.

When water is disturbed, small waves form; in physical terms, it is called the company of others. It is company or friendship to this world but it is a disturbance to the saints. This is why they prefer to stay alone but are never lonely because the creator of the whole universe is always with them. One day you may learn to be alone and enjoy this golden hour here and now. I know God and it also knows me. To me, nothing else matters.

This golden hour may be yours.

THE GUARDIANS

Guru Ji

Guru Ji was the first Master to represent God on earth during the Golden-Age. This line of spiritual Masters is continuous through today and will do so until the end of this physical world. First, God sent five humans to earth, known as the five Princes and Guru Ji was one of them. The reference to the first five humans (Panch Raj-Kumara's) is in Hindu Puranas that are part of the Vedas. This is also my personal experience.

Rebazar Ji

Before we go into the temples and guardians, we must mention our greatest and youngest spiritual Master. He still maintains his physical body and was born in the mountain village of Sarranh in 1461. That makes him 561 years old this year. He is from Tibet. He is approximately five feet ten inches tall, has black eyes and weighs around ninety-five kilograms. His short hair and black beard are cropped closely and he has a very distinctive mark in the middle of his bottom lip. He is eight years older than Guru Nanak, born on 14 November 1469.

He is a messenger for 'The Way to God' spreading the word. He usually reaches the Seekers by direct projection.

His residence is in the western Himalayan Mountains near Tirich-Mir, one of the highest peaks in the world. He wears a knee-length dark maroon robe, always holds a wooden staff in his hand and wears wooden sandals (kharava) on his feet. He has a small mud hut for physical use and there are more saints of similar age or older living nearby, Baba Ji and Kaka Ji.

Other Spiritual Cities

There are nine Dhamas or pilgrimage spiritual cities for the Seekers to visit and learn the wisdom of God. The way to reach these spiritual cities is via spiritual travel accompanied by a living Master. Locations are marked in the God-world chart. These cities aim to provide bases for this planet's magical forces for smooth running and way stations to reach other spiritual worlds.

We all want to get away from the rules, regulations and established orders. It can be done by becoming a spiritual traveller and free to move anywhere within the whole body of the supreme being. This is the truth that we seek here and now.

Damkarh

Banjani Ji is another Master who is teaching here but only to the privileged or advanced students on this path. This spiritual city is called Faqiti, Damkarh, situated in the Gobi Desert. It lies between the highlands of Mongolia and China. During my first visit, Banjani Ji and I stood outside the temple. I noticed that the surrounding area was very dusty, as it happens in dry seasons in India. Damkarh is another outpost of this universe.

It is a large and beautiful city representing the activity of the earth religions. It has splendid cathedrals and holy places where we go to study in Satsang while asleep. Banjani Ji is medium height, about five feet seven inches tall. He has brown Indian skin and long hair combed back very neatly. His beard is a mix of black and grey, as is his hair. He has a special spark in his eyes and it is beyond belief how he expresses the spiritual message through his eyes, known as the Master's Gaze. The expressions in his eyes convey messages very clearly to the Seeker.

Shambhala

It is a place of peace. At present, this spiritual city is embedded in the glacier's ice and peaks about twenty-five thousand feet high. It is near the Gurla Mandhata Peak, which is the highest. This invisible city is the headquarters of the White Brotherhood and is involved in the spiritual governing of this world to bring peace. It is also known as the forbidden land. It is believed that Hindus' original religious Vedas have connections here.

Rahakajah

It is known to us in legend as Camelot during the days of King Arthur. It lies in the southwest tip of England near the seaside of Cornwall. The purpose of this spiritual city is to be the centre for the magical forces of this world. At sunset, some people have claimed to see the mirage image of a spiritual city. To the physical eyes, this place is currently abandoned shipyard docklands.

Satdhama

It is situated in the Pyrenees Mountains, approximately 11,000 feet high in north-eastern Spain. It is on the border of

France and Spain. You will notice all these spiritual cities are in hidden places. Its inhabitants are called the Tulstan Order of the Ancient Brotherhood. They are responsible for the healing purposes in the physical world and other planets of this universe. These mountains are very peaceful and full of wildlife.

Akeveez

It lies in the highlands of southern Guatemala, Central America; the local name is Altos, which means highlands. It is the most beautiful mountainous area, volcanic with clear lakes. Only a few spiritual travellers are connected with this five-thousand-year-old civilisation, the Mayans, which is the link between it and the present world.

Kimta-Vedah

This city is located in South America on the western border of Venezuela and Columbia, in some of the highest parts of the Andes. At present, there are a lot of disputes between these two countries regarding border crossing. It is one of the most outstanding stations that the spiritual travellers have established, other than Agam-Des. Masters here is to keep watch over the planetary spirits and make sure all runs smoothly.

Naampak

This is another spiritual city known as the legendary Rwenjura Mountains of the Moon, in the Republic of Congo in East Africa. This name was given because it appears as two semicircles, like moons, when viewed from the sky. It is very close to the source of the River Nile and it is a very peaceful place comparable to heaven on earth. It is not to be seen by physical eyes, although it is the home of great spiritual travellers, who are responsible for taking care of souls that leave the body at the time of death, especially those who have no one to cross the borders of life and death. They also take care of lost souls due to accidental deaths.

Mumsakah

It is in the southern part of old Georgia, near Russia, hidden away from the eyes of the non-believers. It is in one of the coldest places in the Caucasus Mountains, approximately 18,500 feet high. This region lies between the Black Sea (west) and the Caspian Sea (east). It is situated in one of the world's remote areas, lives the Watchers of the Path, who are the protectors of man's mind. They try to lead our spiritual minds towards God.

Zejirath

It is located near the ruins of Memphis, the temple city of the Egyptians, which went underground over five thousand years ago. This used to be a mighty and beautiful city. Egyptians believe there are many hidden cult temples. Here we find the old faith of that nation, which worships the mysteries of Osiris because these travellers keep faith with the religions and mysteries of the ancient world. They are the keepers of the ancient truths. They were responsible for the pyramids and their positions.

GOLDEN TEMPLES

First Temple: Is located in northern Tibet, hidden deeply in the Thanglha Mountains. It is called Katsu-pari Monastery and is under the supervision of Fubi Kants. At present, Kants is eleven hundred years old and is about five feet nine inches tall as far as I could judge while standing in front of him. He has a dark maroon robe and wears a turban of the same colour; sometimes, he wears pure white clothes. Part one of the golden book is in this white marble temple. Many students are taken to study during their dream state, when they have joined 'The Way to God.'

Second Temple: In this world is at Agam-Desh, the spiritual city in the remote Hindu Kush Mountains, near the Afghanistan and Kashmir border in central Asia. Alexander the Great crossed the Hindu Kush Mountains in 329 BC in this area to enter old Punjab, now Pakistan. This temple is called Garreh-Hira and is under the supervision of Yabal Sakabi. He is over five thousand years old. His appearance is a bald head, dark eyes, dark gold skin and a pleasant smile.

I can say he is about my height. He wears a maroon robe and a rope belt around his waist. Students sit on large rugs when attending classes in the hall. 'Sometimes I wonder how old these rugs will be? It has a platform in the back where the Master stands and Seekers listen. Here upon an altar is the second golden book. My book, The Will of God, mentions this place's other details.

Third Temple: It is in the city of Retz on the planet Venus. It is called the House of Moksh. This temple is similar to an old English cathedral in London. There is a podium from which Master Rami-Noori gives instructions to the Seekers who are brought there to study. He is the guardian of the third golden book. Master Rami-Nuri is tall and well-built with dark eyes and a square face.

Fourth Temple: It is in the Astral Plane. This temple sits in the middle of a green park in the Astral Plane's capital city, Sahasra-Dal-Kanwal. The guardian of this temple is Gopal Das. He is from Egypt but his name is similar to Hindu Indians. The name Gopala refers to Lord Krishna. He is a European look, blue eyes, golden hair that is somewhat shoulder length.

He wears a white robe. This temple is an octagon building of red and white sandstone. It is in the park with eight walkways leading to the centre of this mostly round hall. There is a spheroid mineral block on which is placed the fourth golden book.

Fifth Temple: The Temple of Sakapuri is on the causal plane. It is under the supervision of a Sufi Master, Shams Mohammad of Tabrizi (Iran), who was the Master of the poet Rumi. He is broad and is heaviest in the figure when appearing to anyone on this plane. He usually wears a dark maroon cloak, has long dark hair and sometimes wears white clothes. His eyes are deep brown and he has brown skin similar to Indian or Pakistan origin. He had a very historical relationship with the sun.

During his days on earth, once everyone ignored him or boycotted him to not give fire so he could cook his food, he looked at the sun and said, 'You are Sun and so am I. If you are my friend, provide your heat to my food to be cooked.' It is believed the sun lowered itself till his food was cooked. The fifth golden book is encased in a glass-type casing. Once you read one page, the next page will turn itself for you to read.

Sixth Temple: It is on the mental plane, in the city of Mer-Kailasha. The guardian of this golden book is Japanese Master Sato Kuraj. He is small but has a cute smile when appearing to Seekers. It seems very much like the ancient Temple of Diana, which was in a city on the coast of Turkey. This temple is built in the Greek style and within it is a long, flat block on which rests the sixth golden book.

Seventh Temple: It is in the city of Arhirit, on the etheric plane and is under the supervision of Chinese Master Lai Tasie, who spent most of his life meditating in caves. He is of short height with a long, drooping mustache. His eyes are dark, his mouth is wide but always turned up in a smiling Buddha gesture. The light around him is silvery-white and always accompanied by the sound of buzzing bees and he wears a maroon robe. This building is a great, towering temple with many floors and inside is placed the seventh golden book.

Soul Plane: Sach-Khand: This temple is called Param-khand and it is located in the heart of a magnificent park. There is no community life similar to lower planes because this is the soul plane. We find this golden temple under the supervision of Master Nirgunna Ekom. He is here to guide us to the first manifestation of God, Satnam Ji, where we find Self-realisation. Above, there are golden temples and golden books on each plane, which leads us to experience God-realisation, Anami-Lok and God itself.

HOLY BEGGARS

Beggars are often considered a disgrace to any community or country. These people choose not to work or take any responsibility in life and they feel no shame in putting out their hands to ask for money. I meet a few who are the victims of the circumstances and driven insane by families and they have lost their pride and accepted the attitude of 'Who cares? In some countries, begging runs in families and children are used and trained very early on how to beg.

Now, 'What hope can we have? That one day, they will follow God. The chances are very slim, although they are begging in the name of God. It is strange when you ponder upon their lifestyle. We hear through the media that one beggar died and he had one million pounds in his bank accounts. In India, it has been found that beggars are multi-millionaires. They don't need to beg but it has become a habit for them, which they cannot get rid of easily.

There is another kind and I call them holy beggars. They rob you officially in the name of God and they have registered charity numbers issued by governments. This is a usual practice throughout this world. They are known as saints or priests and it is a known practice in world religions to ask for ten percent of earnings from their followers. People love to donate money to their respective religions, taking it as their religious obligation. Religion is a weakness of humans in this world.

Man has failed to find God within and he uses the external approach, which seems easy. He makes a pilgrimage to some religious temples and within these temples are some statues or pictures representing holy prophets. Most of them know that statues are not Gods but it gives them this feeling and feels blessed.

They hope to carry on in life. Everyone needs to be part of some religion to create an identity and say, 'I belong here.' Otherwise, they will be lost in a wonderland. Very few can stand alone and do something for themselves. Many people make a pilgrimage every year to their respective holy temples. Christians go to Rome, Jerusalem and other places. Muslims go to Makkah. Hindus have hundreds of temples all over India.

I wish God lived in man-made buildings but it is not true. 'Why do you have to travel thousands of miles when God is sitting within yourself all the time? You don't have the time to look within your very home but you can find several days to travel thousands of miles. Throughout their writing, all prophets had expressed that God is within; you simply have to make an effort to experience it. Saints are very few at present and most religions are led by priest-craft.

They are not saints, so they fail to convey the correct message of their religious teachings. Many priests are employed by their religion and trained to ask for donations. All religious TV channels are doing the same. They use these funds to build temples, preach against other religions or destroy the creations of God. These temples become a regular source of their income and these priests play lots of mind games within their organisations to stay put with their jobs.

These holy beggars are living a luxurious life while you live in poverty life. You are the donator and do not realise you are the root cause of the destruction to other people or nations. 'Have you ever realised, what are you doing? Religions are fighting more with other countries than governments. God does not live or reside in temples. Neither is it asking for man-made money. I watched the Indian news on 15 June 2013 and the Kedarnath Dham (a temple) in Uttarakhand and so many other temples.

They were drowned and destroyed by heavy rain, with thousands of corpses lying everywhere. That proves my point written in the last paragraph. Religions are similar to the crawling of a child. The ultimate goal is God and you can only experience it when you begin to walk. Although they claim to be religious, most priest-craft are politically motivated. These temples become indirectly political platforms.

Religious followers come to pray but become political pawns as voters because their priest or forefront saint said so. Often, these saints recommend, guide or dictate to the followers to vote for a particular party. Once most political leaders are elected, they are supposed to run the country. Instead, they come and sit beside some saint's feet for their win and success. If this saint could do this, he should campaign for his position in Parliament.

Asian saints know that they can do nothing, so they take full advantage of their followers. People should not vote for these candidates who rely on these holy beggars. How can they help you or run your country? Beware, all your actions are counted for karma.

IMPORTANCE OF TIME

Time is a unit of measurement to calculate the past, present and future. Without this unit, all the events will pass without recording their presence. Time is our educational factor; otherwise, day and night will appear; we would not know what happened. With Greenwich Mean Time, we can know the time throughout this world. It is the average taken from the earth's rotation from noon to noon. We usually take one full day as twenty-four hours.

Time varies in each country because all the nations cannot face the sun simultaneously. Twenty-four hours turn into months, years and Yugas. Astrologers divide these into several cycles, as described in the chapter on the physical universe. Planets orbit the sun at different speeds, distances and positions and they affect humans to bring good luck and health. There is one principle that supersedes all these effects; Karma.

If we create good karma, it does not matter where these planets are. You will have good luck throughout as the positions of these planets turn in your favour. We often pray and say, 'Please, God, forgive me and help.' Do not ask God or the Master for forgiveness. I will stress this point very strongly. Forgive yourself so that you don't create any further bad karma. Otherwise, new bad karma will turn into many folds, knock on your door and ask you to face it.

Who is responsible for all this? That is only one person; yourself. When you face this payment, known as 'I am going through bad times,' of course you are. 'For how long will you suffer? That depends on your creation and how the payment is being made. We never recognise this as our fault and always try to blame others. 'How long does it take to clear particular karma?

It becomes a cycle measured in years. During this payment, you are caught in a catch-22. When you are trying to make a payment, this chaos pushes you into creating many more and it becomes a never-ending circle or wheel of eighty-four. This is where you need a spiritual Master to lead you out of this mess. He is also limited because he is here to provide guidance and point out the required action but putting things right is your responsibility.

Most of the Seekers are taking years to decide. When you choose to sort out everything, you may be already walking towards a depressed state. We often lose our faith in Spirit or the Master, saying the Master did not help. God can wipe out every soul's bad karma, bad health, negative situations and poverty in a split second. However, then purpose of schooling is lost for the souls. The Master can do the same but you will never learn the lessons. This is where all the religions fail in this world.

They purposely lead the followers into prayers; in my terminology, it is begging for everything. If I am asking everyone not to beg, that means I am of a strong character. So, 'What is your problem? Why can't you be like me? By begging, you lose your self-respect and in this world, you will be kicked about everywhere. 'Why are you praying to God, the Master or statues when God has given you everything equally because it possesses you?

God only wants you to realise, become aware of its' presence and have all you desire. When you come to this condition of living, all your desires vanish. If you want to carry on suffering, that is your free will and I wish you all the best in your sufferings. Turn the clock around and begin to work around your situations. When these bad karmas know that you are knocking at their door, they begin to disappear and your time changes in your favour.

It is only by giving up everything that one gains reality in God. If you care for nothing, you are detaching from worldly things and you will receive gifts from God. Whoever gives all to God receives all from God and you become the assistant. I have been stressing my point many times; learn to give instead of receive. Every second counts. Emotional love leads to attachment, you become a frail person and your lousy time begins.

Our lives are involved around this factor known as time. It is matter, energy, space and time in the lower worlds. Your time in this world begins even before you realise its importance. You don't know who you are in the womb but your mum and dad begin to count the months for your arrival in this world. Your time and date are noted to mark your arrival in this world. Then it is your first birthday, teen years and soon you are an adult.

All the events are recorded until death to mark your departure. Now you see your whole life is based or tied to one factor; Time. Despite knowing the importance of time, we waste half of our lives doing nothing. Most people love their sleep and some have plenty of time to go to the pub for drinking. Ladies have plenty of time to gossip. Although it can be very entertaining at times, the question is, 'What is your spiritual gain out of this?

Other times are wasted on arguments, fighting and jealousy to stop the other person from doing any good. Despite my effort on many occasions to point out the importance of time, Seekers are still on the same railway track. As long as you are glued to your old lifestyle, you will never be happy or progress spiritually. You want to see the whole eternity in a split second of your thoughts, 'What are you doing to materialise your goal?

Time is one of the main factors that dictate our lives. The sun and moon follow time to let us know it is day or night. Clouds act as a shield to prevent sunshine on earth. The earth is always on the move to reach its destiny to see the face of the sun. Can you relate your life to this example? All the stars shine in our galaxy and we admire their beauty. 'Are you shining like them? Why don't you shine so that others can admire you?

Time is so important and short in this life. We live or base our lives on our dreams most of the time. Dreams alone are not enough, try to materialise them; otherwise, there is no success. Why do our dreams not materialise; we do not base our lives on God's will. We often request God to act according to our will. That is when you are praying for worthless things or situations. Mainly there are three types of people living in this world.

First: They are always late. These people make the worst use of their time and I call them the failure type. They will never succeed in their dream projects. Don't be surprised to learn that these people dream the most but fail to execute them.

Second: The people who know the value of time but only manage to materialise some of their dreams. If they cannot gain much, they have not lost either. But it would help if you did more to achieve that plus element.

Third: The most successful people in life. They can project into the future, fully prepared to face new challenges. They put the experience to good use and are in total command. This is why they are sitting in the chair as our leaders. The leadership could be in business, politics or spirituality and people often go to them for advice. You could be this person if you act now.

There is another kind. Some go beyond these classes of people. They have achieved all and now are in control of their time. They spend their time and breathe air as they wish to do. They roam free beyond human knowledge and control their destiny. The past can be used to learn and put into good use to enjoy the present moment. Live in the present moment; otherwise, there will be many tomorrows and you will never catch a tomorrow.

Past and future always give you pain. The past has already gone and you cannot relive it. The future is out of your reach. When you do reach into the future, at that moment, it will be present, so 'Why do we wait for the future when you are already in the present moment? When you are happy, it is not wasted time. In happiness, you create good karma added to your accounts. Time is a gift from God. Use it wisely. Once you have lost or wasted it, there is no recovery.

There are four seasons of the year in our physical universe. These seasons are timed for our physical well-being so that the soul can experience them without any problem. The present moment changes into minutes, hours, months and years. Make sure that you have grown spiritually. Time spent laughing without any purpose is wasted and at the same time, it is another day nearer to the grave. Awake spiritually and then you will choose your day.

In the olden days, every day was our present day because there was no counting in numbers. There was no recognition of past or future. All religions have a special day; Friday for Islam, Sunday for Christians and Thursday for black magicians. Some consider Wednesday a lucky day and other days are used for different beliefs. If we remove name tags such as Monday to Sunday, all days will be the same and lucky. This illusion is self-created by us.

As humans progressed, these numbers or names of days became part of our educational system and we created seven days per week and four weeks in one month. According to the ancient calendar, there were thirteen months per year (365 / 28 = 13). Then the realisation came that each month varied compared to our natural four seasons. That was the reason to alter the number of days each month, such as 30, 31, 28 and 29 days every leap year, to accommodate our longest day on 21 June and our shortest day on 21 December.

Because of these calculations, all four seasons come in similar months and are accommodated within 365 days. These four seasons appear on similar dates every year, but the names of the days change if we study further. There is a time cycle of years when the same day and dates repeat themselves. This pattern is sometimes five, six or eleven years and the leap year repeats itself every twenty-eight years.

Hold on to any happy moment you had in the past; it can help you at present to be close to God. Most of the time, we live other people's lives due to sincerity, obligation, fear or duty. 'By the time you discover yourself, who you are? Your own time is up. Do whatever you need to do but always do it in the name of God so that all your actions turn into good karma. That way, your action becomes creative and time spent wisely.

Every moment brings a change in our lives; it does not mean you are standing still and doing nothing. The reason for listening to other people's dictates is a sign of bad karma. Turn the table around and begin to gain good karma. Be in command of your life as a Master of your universe. The time of your life is limited, so it must be planned what to be done and when. 'What is the time? It is an experience; make sure it is not wasted.

Use your experience for the good of the whole so others can learn something under your umbrella. The present moment is continuous of is-ness. It is like a drop of rain, which disappears in the sand right before your eyes while deciding what to do with it. If we manage to take care of our present moment, the future will take care of itself. Since I was young, I knew time was important, so I planned my life where I should be and at what age.

I achieved my spiritual goal at the age of twenty-eight years. It did not materialise the way I wanted to see it; that was beyond my control. As they say, better late than never, so here I am today. When I became aware that my spiritual goal was not materialising the way it should have been, I set up another goal on a physical basis. I must pack up my working tools at the age of fifty years to spend all my time in the presence of God.

I worked very hard and with the help of Spirit, I accomplished this goal at the age of forty-seven years. I did not hesitate for a day to pack up my working tools. Time is very important. Make plans as you go along or else you will never see the face of God. Most people are saying, 'Forget about God; you will not even see the face of God's angel.' So far, if you have not realised the value of time, it simply means you have not discovered life; that is the reason for your suffering.

Although the present moment is one, you can create two or three out of one if you know how to experience it wisely. That means organised time is time earned; otherwise, it is all wasted. Time is a great healer and whatever came your way as a bad experience will be gone tomorrow. Be the silent soldier of God, who is waiting for you to be its assistant. Desires are known for our suffering. We spend half of our lives planning to execute our desires. If we begin to act now, we can materialise half of them in no time.

Don't daydream, plan and act. The majority of our members are not working and as for living, so they have twenty-four hours for themselves, yet nothing materialising. You should ask your inner self, 'Why? 'Do you know every today is tomorrow for yesterday? So why worry about your past? Leave the past behind and move on with your life. The flowers are ready to bloom in your life. If you have read my book 'The Will of God,' you will know I have left my past behind long ago.

You can imagine the life situation I could have been in at present, physically and mentally. I moved on with the present moment by saying, 'Who cares? That is why I am laughing today. Time is slow for those who wait at the seashore. Time is far too long for those who grieve and far too short for those who are happy and enjoying eternity. Those who are so glad, Christmas is coming soon and last Christmas seems like it was yesterday. Time goes so fast.

I am not simply giving you advice; I have been through every single problem of yours, so you better act and improve your life. All moments of life should be lived because they are coins of gold. You are also golden and your destiny to be reached is also the land of gold. Your creator is waiting for you at the golden temple so that you can receive the word of gold in the presence of the golden man, the first personification of God. When you know you are wanted and waited upon, do you have time?

KAL POWER

What is Kal power? It is negative energy within. All religious writings express the importance of Kal. Kal is the negative pole and it is equal and opposite to the positive, so it is as important as the positive. The whole theory of the lower worlds is based on equal and opposite. Without Kal, nothing can exist. We often do not want to face Kal. This is also Kal because you are holding a negative attitude. If there is no night, the day will carry on forever.

You may think that is good but it will become destructive for the whole universe because the growth of atoms in this world will decrease with time. Kal is looked at as an enemy prospect. I heard remarks from many people; 'Yes, I was doing OK; till Kal power intervened and my life became hell.' 'Is it really? People with these thoughts are believed to be very religious but I don't think they follow their respective teachings.

If their respective teachings emphasise the same, then I will say their prophets had never been above the mental plane. The true picture can only be seen when you go into the soul plane and above and view the lower worlds. Now you will see both sides of the weighing scale. If there is only one side of the scale, this scale will not go up or down. 'If nothing moves in this world, what will be the outcome?

The rising of smoke is as important as the law of gravity. Can you imagine if we threw something in the air and suspended itself there? I am sure you get the importance of equal and opposite. We all want to be positive or lead positive and progressive lives; we often choose routes of negativity to achieve this. What we create during this process will be beyond our control. We are often faced with hatred, jealousy, theft and backstabbing on our part or with the people around us.

Our creations are responsible for suffering. 'What is Kal? We often blame Kal for our failures. It is not Kal that is responsible for all this. These are our self-created situations, conditions and our weaknesses. When we have to face them, we often blame Kal for this. Kal is only responsible for reminding us of our shortcomings.

Our life is based on five passions and we let them run wild. We are responsible for most of our creations and sufferings. The combination of five passions can be called Kal but at the same time, God gave us other qualities known as Chitta, Manas, Buddhi and Ahankar to judge and execute our actions. We can judge and execute all our actions as we go along in life.

God has given us three **virtues.**

Tamas: is the state of darkness or materiality

Rajas: is the state of energy, action and passion

Sattva: is a state of harmony, balance, joy, intelligence, purity and goodness

----

God gave us another **five virtues** to protect us from wrong-doings.

Viveka: how to discriminate between wrong and right

Kshama: how to tolerate and forgive others

Santosha: contentment; this protects us from excessive greed

Vairaag: detachment; or opposite to Moha

Dinta: humility; the opposite to vanity or Ahankar

We have five passions to lead us astray or create wrong-doings and we also have good qualities within to balance our wrong-doings; we often fail to use them. We all are individuals and if we act that way, we can control our actions but we don't see ourselves that way. We become part of the masses and enter the rat race. All our religions are group-based and you are part of that crowd; you do what others are doing. It never occurs to you whether it is right or wrong.

All religions are the leading cause of our failures or sufferings. We are looking for solutions to problems through our religious principles. The action and reaction of five passions and our virtues will land each individual in daily karma and if you don't pay, it becomes your fate karma. Our life or sufferings are based on that, which is our creation. We always blame others for doing black magic on us when there is little truth.

Brahma is the lord of the lower planes and the king of the dead is the accountant of our total karma. If we are responsible for creating karma, then the lord of karma will create situations or they happen naturally to make sure we pay back what we have created. He does not spare anyone. The lower worlds are a training ground for souls via creation, world situations and five passions, so you are bound to create karma.

This creation and paying back is our suffering and learning for the soul. Kal or Brahm makes sure you have gone through every experience possible and explored all negative and positive situations to be an adequately balanced person. Kal is the teacher and you are the student. The sooner you learn this; the sooner life becomes calm and easy to live. For every situation we go through, we are aware that it is for some purpose and we face it with a smile.

The situation disappears quickly with experience in our account. People with positive or spiritual minds guide others to create good karma to eliminate the negative and lead balanced lives. One day you will be a spiritual man to teach others. Many blame God for our sufferings. God is our father and creator, so 'How do you expect your father to punish you? 'Do you punish your children? The answer is within. Create good karma. Kal will help you to learn as a good friend.

Tell others what Kal is? Learn to face the challenges. Kal will smile with you and God bless you because you are ready to be an assistant in the spiritual world. Once you understand Kal, life will be much easier. If you suffer at the hands of others, they are under the influence of five passions and do the worst they possibly can. The lord of karma records their negative actions or deeds. Have patience; they will suffer too.

Many people purposely did wrong against me and I suffered but they are suffering now after many years, whereas I am still around. Kal and positive are both silents; we awake them with our knowingness. Children are so innocent and don't know what Kal or positive is but they always smile. 'Do you know that most children up to the age of three cannot lie? As an experiment, purposely tell them not to touch something in your absence.

When you return, ask them if they touched what you told them not to. If they touch it, the response will be, 'Yes, I have.' At the age of four, their answer most likely will be the opposite. With age, these passions wake up within. It's very similar to a meditation practitioner who tries to wake up Kundalini to achieve psychic powers. With age, we awake Kal within to achieve worldly goods and status. This power leads us to a world of destruction.

Europe is a lot better place to live when compared to Third World countries; people in these countries are suffering for many reasons, the living standard is shallow and there are water and food problems. Kal is not after anyone to make people suffer. We all are after each other to achieve or deceive. Kal is only recording your actions; the reactions will appear later. Someone often said to me, 'Kal attacked,' or 'Kal is after me.'

Kal is not a ghost who is trying to track you down. You are Kal yourself when acting negatively for others or you are in fear. We all act as Kal to each other, knowingly or unknowingly. Each person is frustrated from different angles, so each person is more interested in looking for remedies to their problems and during that, we do a lot of wrongful acts as well.

Kal is a good friend but only if you know it.

MASTER & SEEKERS

We are the creation of God; if there is any first Master, that is Satnam Ji in soul plane. He is the first personification of God. He is the powerhouse for God. He sits between the infinite and the creation of God and he is responsible for all souls. He looks like an American Indian; golden bronzed, shaven head, muscular; about forty years old. He wears bracelets on his upper arms. Everything appears in a golden shade in his presence; he sits upon a huge jewelled lotus with folded arms. He is always in meditation.

The Master is responsible for materialising Seekers' set spiritual goals. Many Seekers are serious and others take everything very lightly. At the same time, they expect heaven to open up for them. It is learned that if any Master is too disciplinary, the Seekers begin to leave him because all the Seekers want a Master to take care of them while they have fun.

All religious temples are based on this theme. We pray to God to fulfil our desires; when our situations are normal, we often forget God and do not feel the necessity to pray. The first knowingness is that you are a soul. We are here to free the soul from the lower worlds, whereas previously you have fulfilled the physical body's needs. This life is a continual succession of spiritual opportunities but we often fail to seize them.

Discipline and spiritual thoughts are the main contributors to having spiritual success. All Seekers cannot become proper spiritual travellers because of a lack of discipline or any seriousness in the teachings they are following. In the same way, it is good to be born in any religion but spiritually, it is not very healthy to remain there. It is good to be born a child; it is bad to stay like a child. To be an assistant of God, spiritual awakening and taking responsibility for each action is a must.

The Seeker must face their weaknesses and conquer them one by one to bring a spiritual life in balance. You must lead an ethical life similar to your Master or as expected by your teachings. Be an example to others. Spirit only enters into pure hearts so that the truth can be revealed. God is within each soul; a few Seekers are pure in their hearts that God uses them as assistants.

As Jesus said, there is no turning back once you put your hands upon the plough handles. The Master said perfection could be given to any Seeker within seconds. A word in the ear is enough, provided the Seeker can grasp and act upon it. The Seekers often fail to maintain their state of consciousness. It will help if you learn to stand back so that the divine Spirit can work through you. Spirit can be experienced live within yourself; that will be your achievement. To experience this, you must have a calm and untroubled mind.

Qualities of the Master

He holds a higher state of consciousness in the inner and his outer actions are always in the name of God. The Master's will is the will of God. Most of the time, he is dwelling in the beingness state, the worlds of pure Spirit. There is no religion, no doors to open and nowhere to go; It Just Is. When the Master gains master-ship, he attains consciousness with God and from there, all his actions are under the direction of the Spirit. He will never be interested in establishing a new religion. This point is easier said than done.

The Master is not a healer and nor does he pose as one but the whole world believes it through mythological stories. That is why people often request healing. Seekers lose the true purpose of following. The Master always rejects any kind of violence. The Master does not obey man-made laws and neither does he break any while living on earth because he is a law unto himself. His approach to all creation is universal.

He is full of love and good health because any person with a disability cannot become an absolute spiritual Master. He is not a slave to anyone and he asks no favour of any man. He always pays for what he gets, creating his living by doing suitable jobs. Spiritually, he is not allowed to live on donations or funds of any organisation. If he does, he cannot be the living Master of the time.

He only sleeps three or four hours daily and can manage to work twenty-four hours without fatigue. Religious leaders are based on the social systems, gathering and praying to seek everything free. These religious systems teach people how to pray; when 'Man is a God' clothed in rags but is the Master of the universe going about material gains for temporary use. Each religious follower is happy to remain within a self-created prison.

The Master may not be educated in a university. Still, he has gone through severe spiritual disciplines or tests, far more superior or more challenging than any education. He does not interfere in the consciousness of any person unless asked; neither does he allows any Seeker to lean upon him; otherwise, the Seeker will never become a Master of his universe. This is why when the Master has shown the way to the Seeker; the Seeker must walk alone.

The Master can do Akashic or soul readings for any Seeker but it serves no purpose for any spiritual advancement. We should be concerned only with the present moment or the continuous of is-ness. When a Seeker's biggest interest is to gain knowledge of past lives; if he has held important positions in previous lives. These are mind-pleasing games and the true purpose of following is lost. The future can be forecasted based on your previous karma.

It is better to build a strong foundation today for future happy living. Aura adjustment or balancing is another fraud business. Your aura is based on your karma, good or bad, reflecting or surrounding your body. Can any person wipe out your karma? Those who do claim are very deceptive people. The craving within for spiritual knowledge or about God leads you to become a Seeker.

We have followed all religious beliefs and tried to memorise all holy verses but nothing leads to spiritual awakening other than surface knowledge. One day you will realise it does not matter how serious you have been; it did not lead to any significant achievement. Most religions don't believe in having a living Master but have complete faith in the Master who lived here a thousand years ago.

These Masters have done their respective duties at that time and have already incarnated a few times in other countries but we still believe they are around. All these ascended Masters have little say in the physical plane. It is similar to that deceased doctor who cannot treat a sick man or a dead mother who cannot provide milk for her child. If departed Masters could take care of new Seekers, there is no need for any new Masters on the physical plane.

God needs one clear channel all the time and this is why so many Masters appeared time after time and will continue to do so. A Seeker in the body must have a Master in the physical body, which is the fixed law. That applies to any educational system. Any request made to a departed Master in the hope that he will help, you will be disappointed because to please you, he will not use lower powers or take physical form.

Neither is he able to because he has incarnated somewhere else. True Masters always pass their spiritual mantle to the new, worthy soul in physical form. Living and being stuck in the past is our failure point. The modern mind does not believe in the living Master but finds no difficulty accepting the story of past Masters who lived a few centuries back. I wonder what education they had; they cannot analyse this simple truth. The living Master of the time will not ask or guide you to go on any pilgrimage to find or seek God.

God exists within each soul as a state of consciousness. The Master guides you to sit wherever you are and meditate to awaken yourself spiritually. There is nothing that you cannot know or understand. All spiritual knowingness and spiritual planes are at your disposal. You are the reflection of a big mirror and there is nothing that you cannot see. In the same way, you see your reflection in the river of God. You will glide like a hawk in the sky upon the currents of Spirit as a free soul and that will be your awareness because you are part of God.

The more you become aware of the light within, the more you know that you are part of God and humbler to all creation. This is the result of self-surrender to the Master and Spirit. You decided to live spiritually free and not in a self-created prison. This is why God created lower worlds and reincarnation systems to explore the whirlpool so that we can learn and one day become assistants in the cause of God.

The present Master is appointed by Satnam Ji, because he has earned the authority to wear the spiritual mantle. He speaks with authority and maintains his state of God-consciousness. Regardless of his state of consciousness, many Seekers believe that the Master is free from physical problems or psychic harm or disease. This is not true. As long as he lives in the lower worlds, he is subject to suffering just like us.

Seeker: who are excited by the spiritual teachings but fail to practice them.
Seeker: who listens to the Master and reads the discourses but is mentally restless.
Seeker: who follows the Master and his teachings, still fail to reach a set goal.
Seeker: who is successful and travelling within but these are very few.

Most of them are stuck in the problem zone. No man has managed to solve life's problems by following any religion or philosophy. It is the realisation of responsibility to clear any negative karma earned already. Now you are making a way in life and achieving your keep and not living off others as you used to do. The Master is here to guide you; he is happy with those who are walking along but he does not look back at who is following or not.

This decision is left with the Seeker and is known as free will. God has granted free will to all souls to learn according to their own pace. The Master is interested only in the spiritual welfare of the Seeker to make sure he makes his castle in heaven. The Master is not interested in self-created problems of any Seeker; This is exactly what he is pointing at to take responsibility for each karma committed. Most humans are thieves at heart and they will try to get away with whatever they can.

The fear of law and not facing imprisonment makes them stay within the boundaries of a safe zone or maintain their good status in society. We are not here in any winning or losing position or for austere practices to eliminate these karmas. As we unfold all of our doings, we balance our karmas. We should pay full attention to the health of the body and the mind. The Way to God's teaching is beyond religion; we cannot sell any material goods such as jewellery, flashy posters, uniforms or anything that all religions are doing.

On the same basis, we do not celebrate the deaths or births of our past Masters. We believe in the present moment and the present Master. All religions are based on past moments, repeating old mythological stories. They forget how to enjoy the present moment and cannot dream of what the future holds. All our Masters live in this moment and this is why they do not have strong human relations. I can sit alone forever and probably I'll be more-happier if left alone.

All physical conversations force me to act like an average human. Sometimes I do feel irritated because of this lost time. No Seeker can serve two Masters and gain any spiritual grounds. The semantics of the two Masters are different, which will act as split attention of the Seeker. That cannot be spiritually beneficial. All Seekers must give their current mailing address if they want to receive teachings, not of their relatives' address.

We would be as guilty as the Seeker if we allow this. This indicates we are not being honest. Many people do this because of certain circumstances in the family and some fear running in their minds. We cannot progress spiritually with fear in mind and dishonesty with ourselves and the Master. The Master does not allow anyone to pray for others or to change their state of consciousness. We must grant psychic space or free will to all.

More harm is done through prayers to others and yourself without the person's permission. Many people try to harm the Master or any spiritual person and these souls live within the protective shield of the Spirit. The cosmic Spirit is a law unto itself, so whatever comes, it automatically goes back to the sender. The sender suffers the consequences. Masters are laws unto themselves and they are only accountable to God.

The main failure point of Seekers is to seek as much knowledge as possible. That is the requirement for the mind. However, success only comes when you stop seeking and clinging to any materialistic thought. All universes are the temple of Spirit and Seekers are its sanctuary. Go within; there is nothing you cannot know or understand. 'Do you know that as you progress spiritually, your facial features begin to change as well?

Self-surrender is very important to the Master and God. The secret of self-surrender is; to be so wholly interested in the Master that nothing else matters. Let this faith grow as; you and the Master are one, walking and talking all the time. The Master will take care of all your required securities. Once you are in harmony with Spirit, all your problems begin to solve and all requests are answered without fail. Your willpower is getting stronger by the day and you can move mountains with a strong will.

Your willpower will also begin to go along with the divine will and now you are a microcosm reflecting the macrocosm. The creed of 'The Way to God' is that all life flows from God downwards to the worlds below and nothing can exist without the will of God. The existence of God is only proven to those who make an effort and live in the higher states of consciousness all the time but it cannot be proven to non-believers.

Masters of this path are against using artificial drugs, hypnosis, yoga or any other means to have self-deceiving experiences. The Way to God is the key to spiritual freedom and it is the key to heaven. Unless you are born again, you cannot see the kingdom of God. The complete transformation from a physical being to a spiritual being is required to have this experience. The Seeker must learn to live on the minimum physical needs.

He can live on a minimum amount of food because his intake will be Spirit. Most of his leisure time is spent in meditation. With spiritual success, the Seeker must be at peace within; if not, he cannot bring peace to others. A Seeker's success is the success of the Master and it has been worth the effort of the Master to discipline the Seeker.

SPIRITUAL TRUTHS

To believe in God is strength
To believe in religion is a weakness
To believe in politics is Kal

God is one; religions are many
So are their struggles

Being alone is a strength; being in a group is a weakness
Being lonely is depression

All humans are karmic sick but don't know how to heal
The Master shows the way but they follow not
Yet they claim to be the Seekers

There is land and sky. In between are your passions
They will take you down under or to God

The one who is, has no name
The one who has a name is not God

Freedom is to live life on your condition
Spiritual freedom is to walk away from this
With your own free will

You can experience God's world while still living
Religions are pointing to this meeting after the death
To which there is no proof

Those who recite too many verses
Are depending on religious words
But not God

Those who follow religion are not religious
I do not follow any religion but I am religious
----
*Do not engrave your goals in the sand; one tide comes and
all vanish*
Engrave your goals on a solid base so that nothing can
shake them
A positive attitude and strong willpower create miracles

We all want God in our lives. We are more interested in
Looking for remedies to our problems but not God

To know God, the biggest obstacle
In the way of true Seeker is
Failing to walk away from religion

Do not thump your foot on the ground
Float like angels in the sky
Your destiny is not far away
----
*Duniya which kamyaab hone vaste, loka naal jurhna
jarurri hai*
Sadh bannan vaste, loka nu torhna jarurri hai. (Punjabi)

139

Those eyes looking at me, evil or with love
I bless them all to let them near me
That is my choice.

The Master plays all the best, melodious tunes
So that followers can benefit spiritually
But the Seekers will only accept, like or follow
that which suits them physically

No person in this world is wrong
Every person can justify their actions
People's actions are based on the situation
They are in or were in

SEEDS OF GOD

Let us take the example of a marigold plant. Although the whole plant is potentially contained in the seed, it requires time to transform into the plant. It is the same way with all universes. God sits within each soul and the soul has to become aware of it. The degree of awareness is known as Self or God-realisation. In all these universes, the whole eternity can be contained in the eye of a sparrow.

Take a close look at this seed. At present, 'Do you see the marigold plant inside? The answer is no.

Inexperienced Seed or Soul

If we put this seed in the soil and water it to provide some moisture, it will help the seed to open up in a few days. Soon it will appear out of the soil not as a seed but as a small plant. With time, it will grow in size and know its existence as Self-realisation. Later, its roots will become stronger and steadfast in soil. With the help of good weather (a teacher), it will produce very admirable flowers. Everyone loves its fragrance and admires its beauty.

The realisation of self as Soul

God-realisation giving fragrance to others

If we keep this seed for one hour in soil and twenty-three hours in outside weather, 'Will this seed grow? The answer is no. We can hold this seed in this condition for the next forty years and it will never grow. It is the same with our spiritual unfoldment. Stay within the moisture of Spirit and you will see the results. You do not have to tell others what you do; your fragrance will pull them towards you. This small example is good enough if you want to grasp my point.

Your sincere effort will never go wasted.

SON OF GOD

This is one of the most famous lines in Christianity; Jesus Christ is known as the Son of God. That is true but it does not mean he is the only Son of God in this world. Every soul created by God has the right to claim this title but this title has to be earned. Jesus was known to be the Son but again, 'To what extent was he successful in his effort? No one knows.

'Who is the Son of God? Any person or soul who can earn good karma and hold similar qualities to God is the Son of God. It is difficult even for the most known saints to fail on this point. It is almost the same as God operates in this world. 'Now the question is, can you manage your life on this basis? Maybe you can maintain this state of consciousness a few times but to retain it for a day or forever is not possible.

Even if an iota of five passions is present in your thoughts, you will fail. Now you see what the requirements are to claim this title. If you study the history of saints at present or in the past, you will find some evidence of one or more of the five passions. My experience in this field shows only the direct representatives can claim this quality but at times even they fail to maintain this consciousness. Now you see how difficult it is to keep this title.

God's qualities are infinite. Here are just a few.

Universal

Any Son of God must have a universal thought or approach to all life forms. To kill another of God's creations is a big sin. Jesus was helping his followers to catch fish in the sea and then eat them as food or to sell for the same purpose. In my vocabulary, any religious guru who does this is not a Son of God. It is not Jesus alone; most of the world's prophets fail on this point. In effect, Jesus Christ himself said, 'I am the Son of man.' Later, Christians changed it into the Son of God.

Freewill

Most of the saints fail on this point as well. They recommend that their followers not leave their teachings and mention several consequences if they leave. Instead of teaching them universal thoughts and saying farewell, they build fear in their minds. So, any saint attached to any religion cannot hold universal thought. Being religious means; you are for or against other systems.

Omnipotence, Omniscience, Omnipresence

This means: All-powerful, knowing and present. 'Can any saint hold this state of consciousness? Not a single saint, because they come for some years to spread the message of God in their ways. Then at the end of their physical life spans, their future spiritual journeys are untraceable. God is omnipresence means now, when all religions dwell in history.

Creator

God created everything, souls and universes. 'Is there any saint in our written history who can create souls? I know what they can do and many of them are responsible for creating or being part of religious wars. They were responsible for killing uncountable human lives. That leads to the suffering of their families and millions of negative karmas committed. 'Can these saints be called the Sons of God?

Giver

God is responsible for the whole creation and provides food and shelter without anything in return. 'Can any saint do this? The answer is no. Instead of giving, they are always asking for donations. These donations are used to run their cult systems. God runs the whole world but never asks for any donations. People are so stubborn that instead of saying thank you, most of them don't even believe that God exists.

It never complains or punishes; instead, it has given us free will to believe or not believe. It makes no difference to God. If we do a small favour to our friends or family members in life and if we do not hear a thank-you within a reasonable time, it upsets us. 'Do we have God's qualities? The answer is no.

Tolerance

It is a known factor that if others are not in tune with us, we are not agreeable to tolerate their presence. There are extremist believers in religions but they're not direct believers in God; to them, their religious leader or saint is God. Many swear at God because they know God does not punish them. As the universal creator, it does not discriminate between believers and non-believers. 'Can any saint do this? As I said earlier, we all are children of God as souls.

But to give the title 'Son of God' to any physical or human is not justifiable. As I used, the words physical and human indicate it is impossible to be the Son of God because God is formless and we can never be so. Or if we are formless, then we will never exist. All the lower worlds are schooling for souls and we are learning to live in its presence. All souls are equal and the only difference is our states of consciousness.

One day we will be aware of God and feel its presence invested within us as souls. Any saint or religion claiming, 'I am the only way,' is untrue. This statement indicates it is not a universal thought and does not allow your free will to choose what you want to follow or tolerate. The bigger the promises, restrictions and followers, the more significant is the deception. God created each soul with the ability to find its way to its creator.

For example, a mother tortoise lays eggs at the beach and hides them under the sand. When the eggs hatch after seventy days, their mother is not there to guide them but they walk straight to the water. Many of them are picked off by eagles or similar birds during this journey. In the physical plane, this is what happens to us. Do not follow any pseudo-master. Any person who listens or follows the dictates of these people is frail and not yet ready to be directly in the presence of God. You are an individual and one day; you can be the Son of God with your efforts.

SPIRITUAL TRAVEL

Practice 1

As you are sitting, take a very close look at the ceiling and pattern of plaster or the shadows of light. You can permanently put some crosses on the ceiling at home, where you practice daily. Once you have visualised, close your eyes and relax by taking a few deep breaths. Put your attention on the third-eye and visualise the ceiling. Now forget completely that you are sitting on the ground.

In your imagination, feel that you are near the ceiling; the distance between the ceiling and your eyes is only six inches and you are looking at the pattern of plaster or the shadows. To make it more realistic, you can try to touch the ceiling with your hands. Repeat this several times if you're not successful on the first attempt. Try again till you're successful.

Practice 2

This time, we repeat the same technique but from a different angle. Take a very close look at the window area and visualise everything nearby. You can choose another location most suitable for your sitting position. Then close your eyes and relax by taking a few deep breaths. Again, focus on the third-eye and visualise the window area as before, remembering all the details. This time you are not going to reach the window.

You will try to **be there** as soon as you possibly can. As you are standing near the window, try to look back at your physical body from the angle of a window or your chosen spot. You can also try to run from your position to the window and then look back at yourself. You can also look at others if it makes you feel more realistic. This is called the Saguna-Sati (instant) technique. It can work in two ways.

Either you are looking at yourself from the window area in the soul body or I will not be surprised if your whole body moves near the window or chosen spot. It is called direct projection if it happens this way, shifting your body to the desired place. The speed of action in this exercise is important and this is why I said run, not walk. Repeat this as many times as possible until successful. May success be yours.

SPIRIT

Spirit is the essence of God. It is the life force for all its creation and without it, nothing can survive or exist. It is the bonding material for everything you can think of. Everything is created out of Spirit. Without Spirit, all universes will be unseen or non-existent; the whole space will appear as a big void and no one will be there to witness it. The first creation out of Spirit is light and sound. Light provides visibility and sound becomes the bonding material.

Light is used as knowingness of God's presence and sound is the communication between God and its creation. Pure light is so clear that everything is seen as non-existent but eventually, it appears as a very light shade of white and then pure white. After Anami-Lok, it appears as very light gold and is pure gold in the soul plane. In the lower worlds, colours change dramatically and it appears like a rainbow in the physical plane. Out of this rainbow, you can create millions of colours.

Pure sound is total silence and you hear the hum out of this silence. In the soul plane, you hear the single note of a flute. In the lower worlds, sounds change according to the vibrations of each plane. In the physical world, it becomes the Sa Re Ga Ma Pa, Dha, Ni, Sa and out of this, all world music is created. If you add all the sounds of this world, it will be heard as a hum. It is the same with colours; if you mix all the colours of the rainbow, you will be surprised to see the result. It will appear as pure white.

TV's whole colour theory is based on this factor; RGB (red, green, blue) and a combination of these three is YMC (yellow, magenta, cyan). Add all these colours and the result will be white. In the same way, everything is created out of Spirit and we see the result in lower worlds, in materialistic forms such as land, mountains, sky, humans and animals. As soon as we leave the lower worlds, we begin to fade away. Humans cannot see if you appear to them in astral form.

The soul plane is the last plane when you appear as a soul and almost look like a physical replica. After that, this identity begins to fade away in the misty worlds of Spirit. Eventually, you will disappear as any kind of identity regarding what you look like at present. You will retain your identity as an assistant of God but you disappear into this big, unseen void of God. The total experience is that everything is created out of Spirit and it merges back into its creator.

Now you see that nothing can exist without Spirit. Spirit holds the balance of all planets, universes and the entire galaxy in place. This pure Spirit becomes negative or positive in the lower worlds, black or white magic and many other examples. Going back to the colour theory, if we add RGB, the colour will be white and the combination of RGB is YMC, which is also white. If we retain YMC, which is equal to white but minus red, green and blue, the result will be black.

Now you see, we can also create a black - out - of white. Spirit is unlimited and very similar to its creator, God. All the saints or prophets fail to know God fully; because you are its creation but not God. God is the creator, Spirit is our lifeline and God breathes through us to show its presence. Beingness is a state of pure Spirit and this is why there are no limits to travelling. Spirit is everywhere and so are you in a being state.

All the lords of higher planes live in a being state and they are so close to God that they are almost pure Spirit. When saints in the lower worlds sit in meditation for a longer period, such as a month, a year or longer, they become channels for this Spirit. As the Spirit flows through their bodies, it nourishes the physical body for its well-being. Many ask, 'How can this be possible? My answer is, 'Why don't you try?

All shadows disappear in pure light and so does all materiality in pure Spirit. All the pains or pleasures are part of the negative Spirit and spiritual freedom is part of the pure Spirit. Humans depend on materialistic security, which is why we moan and groan. Despite all the food facilities, we are always short of food. Birds have no permanent homes but they roam from branch to branch and are happy. The will of God is their security, all the food is provided and they never go hungry.

We are the closest to God and have more means of exploring its worlds. We can achieve anything at our disposal; we have lost our trust in Spirit because our prophets and priest-craft have failed to show us the proper path. Our true security lies within. Spirit is the creator and Spirit is the way. The day you become aware of this, you will know all. Until then, you will struggle as you have done all along.

The temple within is the house of Spirit; due to your materialistic desires, you have rented it out to Kal, the negative Spirit within. Your wishes will never end, which is the main cause of human suffering. These desires create a big void between yourself and the Spirit. You are so close to God and it is so close to you via Spirit. It is through this Spirit that you can communicate with the spiritual Master. Through this Spirit, the spiritual Master shows his presence to all his Seekers.

Those who recite too many verses depend on religious words but not God. They will never experience the pure Spirit until they change their belief practice. External is the reflection of the inner and external is negative or positive, whereas inner is pure Spirit. The end of life should be celebrated with a laugh. You can only laugh if you can fly away with five elements as pure Spirit. Now we know God is everywhere as Spirit and any Seeker when in meditation, becomes the centre of the universe.

There is no holier place than where you are sitting now. Only mortals travel from one temple to another when they can be viewed instantly. Live Spirit is the true temple. The other temples are mind-pleasing only. Spirit is the pure essence of God and this is why it is the life force for all God's creation and is found in every flower of the earth and you as well. Spirit is always with you.

SPIRITUAL CHAKRAS

Indian saints were the first to explore spiritual chakras, so all the credit goes to them. I will write very briefly on this subject because we do not practice these chakras and you can find lots of information on the internet from many yoga groups.

Muladhara Chakra: It is the four-petalled lotus centred at the rectum; the colour is red. It is the seat of the earth element and the first stage of the yogis. The word to be used here is Kaling.

Kundalini: is a pair of snakes lying wrapped or coiled in sleep, waiting for the right concentration to arouse them for Ridhi-Sidhi powers. It centres between the Muladhara and Swadhishthan chakras.

Swadhishthan Chakra: It focuses on the reproductive organs and represents the creative powers. The colour is orange and it is a six-petal lotus. It is the water element and the second stage of yoga. The word repeated here is Onkar.

Manipurak Chakra: It is the eight-petal lotus. The colour is yellow and it is the seat of the fire element. Located opposite the navel in the spinal cord and it represents the sustaining and nourishing power. The Manipurak chakra is the third state in yoga and the word repeated is Hiring.

Anahag Chakra: It is the twelve-petal lotus. The colour is green. The Anahag chakra is focused on the heart centre and represents the destructive power. It is also the breath centre and the seat of the air element. The word to be used here is Sohang.

Vishudha Chakra: It is the sixteen-petal lotus. It is concentrated at the throat and is the seat of the ether element. The colour here is blue and the word the yogis use for repetition is Shring or Ashtang.

Do-dal Chakra: It is the two-petal lotus and is indigo in colour. It is located behind the two eyes and is the sixth stage of the yogis. Do-dal is ruled by the mind element and is opened by a repetition of the word Aum. It is also known as the pituitary gland or the seat of the mind.

Third-Eye Chakra: This is the true chakra, known as the seat of the soul. Spirit enters through the Crown-Chakra to be in contact with the pineal gland and reach all lower chakras. The word to be used here is Haiome.

Crown-Chakra: It is like a way station to have any success. Without this centre, Spirit cannot enter into the body or any lower spiritual centres. It is known by many names; 'soft spot' or 'narrow is the way.' It is very similar to a bottleneck and a bottle can be filled or emptied through this opening.

Medulla Oblongata: It is situated very close to the pineal gland. It is at the beginning but the rear point of your spine. This is another spiritual centre to do soul travel. The attention is focused mainly on the back wall or three to four feet behind you. You can use any spiritual word for practice.

When your outer world has been closed and inner world of thoughts and attention is fixed unwaveringly at the third-eye, you are ready to step across the invisible veil between the objective and subjective worlds. You should lose all feeling and sensation of the existence of the body.

SPIRITUAL LIFE

During one of our meetings, I advised everyone to work hard and spend as much time achieving their spiritual goal. A newcomer asked, 'How would you summarise the whole lecture in one sentence? My answer was, 'To live your life as directed by God.' These eight words can be your life-changer but otherwise, we can write another holy book to explain. 'The question is, are you living your life as directed by God?

There are thousands of religions in this world and have billions of followers. Of these billions, probably a few thousand live their lives as directed by God. Others follow the dictates of their religious systems, which are misleading in hundreds of ways. Most of them lead lives as directed by the mind, not God. They are so occupied in the turmoil of mind games; they fail to differentiate between religious and spiritual.

'Do you know all religious followers believe that they are living the life as directed by God? But they are not. All holy books express the truth experienced by the prophets. These prophets no longer live; their teachings are turned into a religion. Religion is a system to follow and at the head are priest-craft. Any priest can read the holy book but he is not the knower of **truth** experienced first-hand by the prophets.

Priests are not saints; it is an adopted occupation to earn a living. Behind this occupation, lots of deception is carried on to mislead followers. This is done purposely to keep their jobs. If this person leads a life of deception himself, 'How could he guide you to live your life as directed by God? They use all the tactics to create funds; 'God does not want any money, so who does?

Some of the funds are spent on building temples. 'Is God living in these buildings? Spirit is the essence of God, which can be experienced at any time with the power of creativity. Most of the funds are used against other religions to create holy wars. Many countries have been destroyed and millions have lost their lives.

Due to this, their spiritual experiences are at a halt. 'Who is responsible for this? They are our religious leaders and these people with devious minds have hatred for other religions. 'Are they going to teach you how to live your life as directed by God? They are lost individuals in their lives in many ways; otherwise, they would not be living at the expense of others. If you become an extreme follower of any religion, you are a failure in the eyes of God because you are for or against other religions or souls.

You have moved one step away from the workings of God. You have created a wall between yourself and the rest of the creation. 'Will God accept you as its near or dear one? Ask this question to yourself. It does not matter what you follow to know God's ways; you must hold a universal approach to the rest of God's creation; love all its creation as you love God. None of the religions at present hold this universal approach.

Christians provide door-to-door service on Sunday to increase their following. Islam believes in the conversion of this world into one religion. They have one good approach to believing in Allah, not worshipping any idealism of prophets or statues. That is a direct approach to God but other than this; their approach is not on neutral grounds. Many holy wars are being fought, known as jihad. We cannot expect the whole world to become one.

God has created each soul individually to gain spiritual experience. Free will is the key to spiritual success. God does not interfere in our right or wrong actions; our mistakes are taken as our experiences in life. 'Who are these religions and their priest-craft to dictate the lives of their followers? They all are against the individual thought of living. Those who don't follow are known as non-believers or Kafir. I love this word Kafir. 'Do you know why? Because the whole world is full of Kafirs.

It does not matter what religion you follow; it applies to every religious person in this world because no one approaches God directly. All religious followers are interested in the intermediates, known as prophets or gurus. They all fail to see the mirror. When you see yourself in the mirror, you will only know your true looks. Otherwise, everyone believes that they are pretty. Ninety-nine percent of the population of this world is in the deception of true belief.

Only God can decide if you are following his ways. All religions say our holy book holds a higher truth than others and our customs and costumes are better. Our prophet is the only one who has been closer to God or sent directly by God. Many mythological stories are created to prove that it is the only truth. He is the Son of God. We are souls of God, created individually to experience the lower worlds and face five passions of the mind, controlled by the negative force.

One day we may become the assistants in God's world. All these religions and their followers are under the dictates of Kal power. They are misled into believing that whatever they are doing is the will of God. I wish we all stood clear from our religious beliefs and viewed ourselves on a neutral basis to know the truth. I talk to many people this way and the usual remarks are, 'We never taught this way,' but it does make sense to all open-minded people.

Now at least they know; one day, they will apply this principle in life, face reality and are one step closer to God. Before, they were miles away from God, although at times they felt are doing God's work, not knowing their approach was opposite to what God expected of them. Half of the animal kingdom is created in a way to kill or be killed by others to experience life. Half of the animal kingdom is based on vegetation living.

Humans have already gone through this experience and with spiritual unfoldment, they are one step closer to God. This is the difference between the animal and human kingdom. By now, we should be the caretakers of the animal kingdom to assist God as co-workers. Most religious leaders and followers are slaughtering the creation of God. Yet, they believe they are God-loving people and do lots of charity work when true charity is lost.

Live and let live is the key to success. In all creation, all living things have the right to live in this world as they wish. You may be surprised to learn that many religions don't believe that animals have souls; if you are one of them, that is why you are still part of the Kal team. I illustrate an example to prove that there is very little difference between yourself and the knowingness of animals. They have very similar feelings toward their children.

I watched a nature program on TV, as I do most of the time. I believe there are many facts of life we can learn from them. It was called 'Savannah, The journey in Africa by David Attenborough. There was a herd of elephants. I noticed most of their calves were walking in the middle of the grown-ups. They walked many miles toward their destination during the drought season to find water. One of the calves fell sick during their journey due to the lack of water and mother's milk as nourishment.

The mother was weak and starving herself; the baby began to crumble. The rest of the herd kept moving but this calf's mother stayed with her child. Throughout this ordeal, the mother protected and kept watch over her child, sensing the poor health condition. She saw and felt the last breath of her child and once she was sure that her child was no more, only then did she move on to find her herd.

During this whole experience, I felt that the animals understand the value of life more than we humans do. 'Now, you call them animals and say they have no soul? There are millions of farmers throughout this world and it is their business to raise animals for slaughter and then supply them to chains of stores.

Yet they all go to church on Sunday and some go on Friday to ask for forgiveness. 'Who are they deceiving, God or themselves? For sure, their actions are not directed by God. Many religious days are celebrated by killing animals, known as Bali, which means sacrifice. Eid is celebrated in Islam and involves the sacrifice of animals. Sacrifice to Kali-Mata in Hinduism and many tribes in the African continent.

The followers of Sikhism believe that they can eat meat because their last guru ate meat during his struggle with the

Mughal Empire. Probably it was a need due to the circumstances they were living in. I don't argue with these people because they will find another excuse to win the argument. I go one step further. 'Can you name any of the gurus who drank alcohol? All ten gurus lived very ethical lives and set hundreds of examples for how to live our lives as directed by God.

Not a guru drank alcohol, so why do their followers drink it? They are all misled not by the gurus or their religious books but by the priest-craft living similar lifestyles. Looking into the facts and figures at present, we should not expect any pity from this world regarding the animal kingdom because they don't even spare humans. The war between Sikhs and Muslims started four hundred years ago and thousands of people lost their lives on both sides.

It is sad to know people are still losing their lives at the India-Pakistan border every day. Power and hatred are responsible for this in the name of religion. Young and innocent boys are brain-washed and fully prepared to become suicide bombers. Yet every Muslim goes to Masjid on Friday and prays to Allah. I am not pinpointing Muslims; this is the routine practice of most religions. Hindus are not saints in many ways.

Once India was known as the most religious place on earth, people visited here to experience spiritual feelings. It is full of negativity, crime, rapes, greed, power, etc. Those who don't believe in God are called atheists but they are better than religious followers in many ways and I believe they are closer to God because they can avoid many wrong followings. If we study most religions, we can probably find no fault in their prophets or holy books.

161

But the followers fail to follow how to live their lives as directed by God. Very few are lovers of God, whereas others are God-fearing, knowing their weaknesses and wrong-doings. They only follow religion to believe that they are protected from their wrong-doings. You will notice they only go to church or temple to ask or pray for forgiveness. 'Why do you have to ask for forgiveness and stand in shame in front of your creator? You should not be doing any wrong act in the first place.

God provides many opportunities in our lives to make our turning point. God forgives as we forgive our children. Analyse all your actions in the future and ask, 'Are these God-directed or mind-directed actions? The answer is always within us. After some time, practice becomes a habit of no wrong-doing. Now, all your actions are directed by God and you can lead others to do the same. This world can be similar to heaven if we allow it to happen. Now you are living your life as directed by God.

SPIRITUAL SIGNIFICANCE
OF NO; 5

All known saints have used; five as a primary number because it represents God in many ways. Most of the creation is based on this number.

Sach-Khand: The soul plane is the fifth plane from this physical world.

Humans: When this world was ready for human occupation, God sent the first five saviours to this earth. They are known as the five Raj kumara's in Hindu Vedas.

Humans have five bodies to use, one on each plane, to achieve spiritual freedom.

Human body has five main parts: A head, two arms and two legs.

Humans depend on the number five. We have five fingers on each hand and foot.

Humans are created with five elements: Spirit, water, fire, air and earth.

Human life is controlled by five passions: Lust, Anger, Greed, attachment and vanity.

We have five senses: taste, touch, smell, sight and hearing.

We have five virtues: wisdom, love, truth, goodness and justice.

We have five tastes: sweet, sour, bitter, pungent and salty.

There are five continents: Europe, Asia, Africa, Oceania and America.

The Olympics has five rings to represent each continent.

There are five oceans: Pacific, Atlantic, Indian, Southern and Arctic.

God created five races of people: white, black, brown, red and yellow.

God created five life forms: humans, animals, birds, sea life and plants.

Canada has five great lakes: Erie, Huron, Michigan, Ontario and Superior.

Punjab, India, has five rivers: Sutlej, Beas, Ravi, Chenab and Jhelum.

China has five sacred mountains.

Sikhism; The tenth Guru created Sikhism. He chose the first five loved ones.

He gave five K's to Sikhs: Kesh, Kangha, Kashhera, Karha and Kirpan.

Five virtues: truth, kindness, contentment, humility and love.

Sikhs have five seats of authority; Golden temple, Damdama Sahib, Keshgarh Sahib, Hazur Sahib and Patna Sahib.

Islam: They pray five times daily.

Five pillars of Islam: faith, prayer, charity, fasting and pilgrimage to Makkah.

Jewish; The Torah contains five books.

There are five books of Moses.

Christianity; There were five wounds on Christ.

The number five is used 253 times in Bible.

Buddhism: They have five commandments.

You will not kill or harm living things.

You will not steal

You will not have wrong relationships.

You will not tell lies or speak unkindly.

You will not drink alcohol or take drugs.

Jainism: They have five bows.

Ahimsa: non-violence

Satya: truthfulness

Asetya: receive no free lunch or gifts

Brahmacharya: No adultery

Aparigraha: avoid excessive attachment

They have five colours on their flag: white, red, orange, green and dark blue.

They have five supreme beings: Arhats, Siddhas, Acharyas, Upadhyayes and Sadhu.

Hinduism; uses five items during a wedding ceremony: flower, coin, durva grass, turmeric and rice.

Naag panchami is the worship of snakes on 5 Sawan (July/August) every year.

Generally; A star has five points.

A starfish has five arms.

The number five is considered a sign of freedom.

The five-pointed star represents the planet Mars (Mangal), which is considered lucky.

Five is the first digit to form a circle.

TO BE OR NOT TO BE

William Shakespeare wrote the title of this section in **Hamlet**. It is well said and applicable to all spiritual Seekers. It is time to make a decision. Do you know that most people cannot decide from birth till death 'What they want to do in life? They follow the family pattern of living and they feel successful. You need to walk out of this system, decide as an individual soul and set a goal for yourself. This goal should be something of a unique nature.

By leaving this world, you should be able to say, 'Yes, I have done something I wanted to do and am successful.' I set up my goal very early and am successful, yet I feel I could have done a lot more if somehow, I had a better platform to stand on or work. After my success, I still have to face the negativity expected as long as we live in this world.

My advantage is that at least I can understand and bypass many situations with the help of Spirit. One of the main problems of a spiritual Seeker is age and responsibility. Everyone wants to experience God in this life but people are not interested in God. They are seeking quick solutions if somehow, they can perform miracles. This is to satisfy their minds and tell others how extraordinary they are.

It is all illusion thinking because it will not work that way or quickly. You have to lay a solid spiritual foundation to do these things. If your spiritual foundation is strong, you don't have to create miracles to impress others. Miracles will happen of their own accord. I purposely do not create any miracles but Spirit creates many miracles on my behalf. People come and tell me how and what they have seen.

It is nothing of my own doing; this point was cleared long ago by Jesus Christ upon asking about many miracles. He replied; of my own, I do nothing. The Father does all and he says something in this manner. I don't think any true saint purposely tries to create miracles to impress the followers. If you do, there will be some price to be paid by going through some kind of suffering. Only magicians create elusive magic to earn their living.

All young followers have one thing in mind; I am still young. What is the big rush to become a severe spiritual Seeker? Although they are still following, they find many avenues on the side. Some are good and many can derail them. Time goes on and these other avenues multiply. Some are part of increased responsibility with age and many cling to our wrong-doings. There is always some nudge from the Spirit but you cannot shake them off.

Some have become a part of you until your last breath. The question remains the same; 'To be or Not to be.' You wanted to **be** something but can you add this one word **come** with it? To execute your dream, you have to **become** what you wanted to be original. We kept repeating these few words but failed to compromise with them. We are so busy that we consistently forget to find the time.

These few words are applied in all fields; spiritual, business or politics. We set our goal and begin to work around it as required. In business, you can see some growth in time, which will build up self-confidence. Business can be done with honesty and it may have slow growth. Many people use negative traits to find success. Politics is the same. You carry many negative or deceptive traits; otherwise, it will not be called politics.

It is much easier to become a prime minister of any country than to become a true saint? A saint is a symbol of purity. You have to pass through challenging tasks with slow progress. Any proper saint will never have the courage to declare that he is spiritual because he knows that there is much more to learn and achieve. The more he succeeds, the more humble he becomes and states to people that he is no higher than anyone.

People around him experience the difference and praise his state of consciousness. It is tough to find a true saint in this Stone Age, although at least one million people claim to be saints. Most of them are fake or pseudo-masters; they all are after making money. 'Do you know; if you want to make quick and easy money, you should claim to be a saint?

You don't have to do anything; people will come in flocks with cash. Although they all want to make money, they believe that you will help them make quick money. Many famous saints in India are behind bars for their wrong-doings. They were all criminals and were running criminal activities with the help of politicians, boosted by their followers, who were poor and were looking for a shoulder to lean on.

These criminal-minded people take advantage of your weaknesses. They are now serving long terms behind bars, charged with murder, rape, robbery, abduction, money laundering, etc. Now, why did we mention these people in this chapter? Because they were claiming to **be** saints and failed to **become** saints. These people give a bad name to spiritualism and people lose faith in God.

The original question remains; 'To be or Not to be? It is tough to make a decision in life and execute it. Jesus Christ also mentioned wolves disguised as sheep. It isn't easy to judge because of their appearance, making them look like saints. Spiritual Seekers must make up their minds. Lead your life because we all have to live in this world but priority must be given to our goal; to experience God in this lifetime.

I heard someone say, 'Yes, I am sure. I will be more serious in later years.' I wish it could work out that way. With age, we have more responsibilities, worries and ill-health. Even if you try to fulfil your goals, I am sure you will face many disappointments. We dream about our set goal but have failed to execute it.

Making a core decision in life is one of the most challenging. For those who do decide, God does not fail them. The obstacles will be many but nothing can stop those who want to dwell in the ocean of love and mercy. To **be** is a question but to **become** is your decision. Once you become fully realised, you learn that you only wanted to be similar to your creator God. Be yourself and let the others be.

You will dwell in the heart of God.

VICTIMS OF THE CIRCUMSTANCES

Most famous people have been the victims of the circumstances, such as Jesus Christ, Guru Arjan dev of Sikhism and others. When you are a victim of the circumstances, that completely changes your life's destiny. Your suffering is inevitable and beyond your control and life is wasted. 'Will you ever be able to turn the clock back? May the Spirit be with you. Guru Arjan dev took the circumstances created by Muslims as the will of God.

Later, gurus stood up against these circumstances and out of these circumstances, a new religion formed from Hinduism, known as Sikhism. There are so many wars and civil wars within countries, a few power-hungry people or politicians create the situations and the amount of destruction is beyond imagination. This will destroy tremendous amounts of property, which they cannot replace for several years.

Human lives are lost, families are destroyed and all these people who leave their countries and take refuge in safe countries become refugees. These people are victims of the circumstances. Sri Paul Ji was very successful in spreading the message of God and some religions felt the threat. He passed away a lot earlier than expected. The circumstances of this spiritual path changed. A new Master took over and later; he passed the spiritual mantle over to another Master.

I was the future of some organisation but I have been a victim of the circumstances due to that, nothing materialised for me. There is a saying; if two birds are tied together, although they have four wings, they cannot fly. I feel the opposite. I am free as anything but I always felt that my wings had been clipped. It means I can make an effort to fly but I never will.

Despite having a higher state of spiritual consciousness, I failed to be recognised by many people as a saint. When looking at my failure, I take it as the will of God but at the same time, I know it is not true. Many people come to me crying for help and their stories are very painful. I tell them to create good karma to improve their lives. Some create the circumstances, while many are the victims of the circumstances created by their friends or families.

I know well-educated people, well-defined bodybuilders and so many other able people unable to succeed because they are under the shadow of others who are more influential. These people become the victims of the circumstances. Mrs Hillary Clinton is brilliant and capable of becoming America's president. First, she was the wife of Bill Clinton; once he made a statement that his wife helped him be a better president.

She supported Mr Barack Obama for some years. In 2016, she tried again to fight the presidential election against Mr Donald Trump. She was more intelligent than him but was not accepted as the first female president; she lost the election in November 2016. She became the victim of the circumstances and I don't think she will try again because she will be too old by the next election. It does not matter how but we all are victims of some circumstances.

During the early eighties, the Indian government played its political game and placed one of their important person in Punjab so that the Congress party could have a stronghold in that area. This person was very religious; once he realised the truth, he backfired at the government. That led to the destruction of the Golden Temple in Amritsar and it was followed by the assassination of the prime minister of India, Mrs Indira Gandhi.

Once the news spread that Mrs Indira Gandhi was no more, her body was kept for three days so that people could pay respects to her but at the same time, this party ordered their followers to carry out the massacre of Sikhs in Delhi. This also carried on for three days. I arrived in India on 28 October 1984 and she was assassinated on 31 October 1984 and I happened to be in Punjab and Delhi area at that time.

The Government figures were very low, but over ten thousand people were killed. Later more than sixty thousand youth lost their lives through fake encounters in Punjab. This only stopped when US President Bill Clinton intervened and made a very small statement to the effect 'I think Sikhs are suffering in Punjab' then India Government got the message and everything stopped overnight. All these people or families became victims of these political circumstances.

These families are suffering until today and no justice has been given. Those who persuaded Mrs Indira Gandhi to attack Golden Temple are roaming free and visiting the golden temple. I always sympathise with the victims of the circumstances because most are innocent people. Their karmas are being mixed up with unknown people, which is beyond their control.

India and Pakistan are firing on the border every day. If you watch the news on both sides, they blame each other. I know both sides are not saints. The political leaders are more interested in maintaining their status and to do that, many people die. Do they care? I don't think so. It is the same story in a few Islamic states.

North Korea and America are doing the same. Nothing has happened yet but they are on the verge of creating something similar. I will call these self-created circumstances, which will harm so many in the future.

VILLAIN OR SAINT

Ravana of Sri Lanka, Doryodhna of India and so many others are the names of frustration. A saint can turn into a villain and the most prominent villain can turn into a saint. When you are extremely negative or positive, that can become your turning point in life. A sage person can turn highly foolish and any foolish person can turn into a wise man. Many people believe that I am successful physically and spiritually but I have been through many failure points, which could have turned me into a villain.

God and Satnam Ji kept me in balance and because of them, my clock kept ticking in the right direction. I can understand the frustration of others who have turned into villains. This is why my sympathy is always with them. I hope the clock can be turned back for them; they could have lived decent lives. Once you are tagged as a villain, you will be known as such forever. We will discuss the background of such people very briefly.

King Ravana of Sri Lanka is known as a famous villain in Hinduism. 'Was he a villain? Or has the Hindu religion believed it as such and at present, priest-crafts talk about it, only telling half the truth to their followers. No one takes the side of Ravana or talks about his goodness. Ravana was the most educated in religious studies; he was a great scholar of the Vedas and worshipper of Lord Shiva. The foundation of the war between Sri Ram and Ravana was his sister, Shurpanakha.

She was the main character and the cause of this war between them. She fell in love with Lakshmana, the younger brother of Sri Ram. Lakshmana got angry; that was his character in life as an angry young man. He cut the nose of Shurpanakha and she complained to her brother, King Ravana. Then the king got angry at this insult and he planned something similar to teach them a lesson. He abducted Sita, the wife of Sri Ram.

Lakshmana could have told her politely that he was not interested. People often condemn Ravana but his actions can be seen as a reaction to the mutilation of his sister's nose. War began. 'Who started it first and who is the villain? To love someone is not a crime. There are ways of coming to some other conclusion. The base of the story is that; Sri Ram's father, King Dasharatha, was married to three women simultaneously. It was the deceitful doings of Sri Ram's stepmother, Kaikeyi. Due to her doings, they ended up in exile.

If Sri Ram, Sita and Lakshmana were not in exile, this situation would have never occurred. We often overlook and point the finger at others to make them look like villains when the actual culprit is sitting right under our noses. All Hindus burn the statue of Ravana every year on Dussehra day and celebrate their victory.

Was Ravana a villain? 'Who was responsible for making him one? Although Ravana was a highly religious person, sometimes it is tough to control or balance the flow of Spirit, which can turn into anger. Sri Ram was also a victim of the circumstances created by his stepmother. Second, the fury of his brother Lakshmana led to a big war. King Dasharatha, the father of Ram, also died in the shock of Ram's exile for twelve years.

The root cause of destruction was Kaikeyi, not Ravana as believed. Ravana and all others were the victims of the circumstances. 'Did you ever notice that true villains often walk away from the situation and innocent ones are trapped to suffer for generations? I still am a victim of the circumstances and I cannot talk about it openly. 'Do you know why? Because it is all backfiring on me, the innocent party. Now, what can you do about it? Nothing.

There are so many fake villains known as pseudo-masters and pretending to be saints but their motive is to gather money and make a chain of properties; they have no shame. These people commit extreme acts and end up behind bars. There are so many saints in prison in the modern era for example, Baba Asa Ram, Baba Ram Rahim, Rampal and so many others in India. They had millions of followers visiting them every year and in the eyes of their followers, they were Gods.

They abused their trust and people lost their faith in these 'Masters' and walked away from religion and their belief in God. Their assets are in the millions of US dollars. If you are a saint, people do take advantage of you. You are humble and in most cases, Spirit doesn't help either. You are doing your best but no one is protecting your back.

The insults you receive are unbearable and leave scars on your life forever. Anything can trigger you to be a villain. Then some bandits take full advantage of your weakness and rob you of everything. If you have any pride or goodness left in you, they will shatter it into pieces and there is nothing you can do about it. Again, there is no backup from Spirit. You can do nothing except hope that you will succeed in your mission and everything will be ok one day.

When you can't reach the goal, the grapes are sour; as the saying goes, failure is at your doorstep. There are so many who will hold grudges and anger against you; that could be the result of your success or your decency, which they cannot tolerate. They could be normal or good people but their failures push them to become villains because they have nothing else to do. When you know these people cause your suffering, it stirs anger to turn you into a villain and take revenge.

There is always something going on to stop you from taking any such action. Although you suffer, still Big Brother is not watching your back. 'I often wondered why and what was I getting acting like a saint? I suffered all my life but still, I have not received any decent or solid answer. I often ask, 'Is all this really worth it? At present, I am not satisfied with my achievements. I suffered extremely and villains are still roaming happily.

Who will justify this suffering and punish the culprits? We believe in karma but it may occur when you are not around; if karma is not served in your lifetime, it has no value and many disappointments. I sometimes wonder whether it is worth becoming a saint in the future. I may decline any such assignment in the future. Many times, you ponder upon it and become a villain as well.

Another example; is who did become a villain in the eyes of his people, although fighting for his throne, which was rightfully his in the first place. This is the story of Mahabharata, another Hinduism epic. It is regarding the throne of Hastinapur, UP, India, 3139 BC. There were three brothers; Dhritarashtra, Pandu and Vidura (a half-brother). The eldest, Dhritarashtra, was born blind and the throne was passed over to the second in line, Pandu.

Although Dhritarashtra was not happy about this situation, he could do nothing. Pandu should have been made the caretaker until the son of the blind king grew up to adult age. King Pandu was in the jungle and died at a very early age and his five sons were also young. The throne came back to Dhritarashtra (blind king) again. His eldest son, Duryodhana, became the rightful prince and heir to the throne and he began to take responsibility.

At the same time, Pandu's sons were also grown-up and they began to claim back the throne, which at one time was their father's, with the help of Lord Krishna. Krishna played all the tricks in the book and misguided Duryodhana several times. For example, saying not to go naked in front of his mother; otherwise, not even a hundred Pandavas could kill him. The myth is; that if he went naked at midnight in front of his mother, Gandhari, who had Siddhy (psychic) power, then he would receive a boon for protection and live forever.

That was part of the spiritual ritual. Krishna was directly responsible for the defeat and death of Duryodhana and many others I could name but this is not the main discussion. The question is, 'Was Duryodhana, a villain? I don't think so. There are specific rules in royal families that have to be followed. There is a law in England (Regent 1937) that any future king cannot marry any divorcee; if that is the case, his throne will be passed over to another deserving royal family member.

Will Prince Charles be the future king? He is married to a divorcee; therefore British throne may directly be passed over to his son, Prince William, from Queen Elizabeth II unless they change the law. The same thing happened in 1936 when King Edward VIII married an American, Mrs Wallis Simpson, who was already a divorcee. He did not want to leave her and he abdicated himself to France.

The throne was passed to the present queen's father, King George VI. Otherwise, the history of the current royals would have been different. This example is related to Mahabharata's story. Blind King Dhritarashtra and Prince Charles are in the same situation and so are Prince Duryodhana and Prince William. The British throne will not be passed over to the queen's second son, Prince Andrew.

Queen Elizabeth II, whom I respect very much because she lived all her life ethically and did her duty with full responsibility. She has gone through rough patches in life. She is the mother of four children and three are divorcees. It is such trauma in life, being so powerful yet unable to do anything about it. She has been the victim of the circumstances.

During all wars, millions of people (soldiers) die while fighting to achieve justice for their nation. Or are these political games? All these soldiers are stuck in a catch-22. They have to follow the instructions without questioning but once they die, their families suffer and no one wipes their tears. 'Do you know they were the primary breadwinners of their families? They were not villains but made to fight like villains.

Whoever kills another is not a saint; its cause does not matter. Krishna said or it is the belief of Hinduism, that he comes in every age to establish righteousness when things go out of control, karma-wise. These are all mythological stories and there is more mythology in Hinduism than religion. 'Where was he during world war1 and 2 when millions of people lost their lives? 'Where is he now to provide justice to Ukraine victims?

Why did he not come to kill Adolf Hitler and so many other dictators? And there are so many living dictators at present. You will notice that majority of the followers are naive and take these statements as their bible without question. If you do question, the priest will tell you another hundred stories to make it look like the whole truth. By having a wrong belief or following with blind faith, you are the villain to yourself because you have closed the curtains to face the truth.

People believe that religions are important but many don't know that all religions are man-made. All the extreme personalities come out of religions, which are dangerous to other religious practitioners and the general public. All suicide bombers come from some religion in this world. Now we look at another example. Ratnakar was a bandit from a very young age and he murdered so many people before the age of thirty. Dramatic changes came into his life and he decided to become a saint.

He is known as Balmiki and he is the author of a religious book called the Ramayana. He looked after the wife of Sri Ram when Sita was separated from him and she gave birth to his two sons, Luv and Kush. Balmiki was also the guru of Luv and Kush. Now you see a villain can also become a saint and history is full of examples. Ashoka was also power-hungry and killed so many people himself and with the help of his soldiers.

Once he saw so much blood, he realised he should lead a religious and ethical life. After thoroughly examining many religions, he decided to become a Buddhist. Originally, India was called 'Jambudvipa' or 'Indus.' He changed its name to 'Bharat' and later Indus was changed to India. If we take the example of Ashoka and Ratnakar, this complete transformation can take place in one lifetime for any person if destined to do so.

'Do you know most famous prophets had been involved in wars, yet we call them saints? As far as I am concerned, if any guru strikes another to kill, it does not matter what the circumstances are at that time; he is not a saint. The followers are happy but you cannot justify karma's committed. The person you killed was another soul and God does not permit anyone to kill any of his creations. As they say, God is closer to you than your heartbeat or breath.

That is the difference between Villain and a Saint. In Iraq, Mr Saddam Hussein was the villain to his people. Then super-villains came and killed him and thousands of people died who were the victims of the circumstances. It is a belief in Sikhism that the tenth Guru Gobind Singh and Aurangzeb used to meditate together in one of their previous lives. When they came face-to-face in their last historical lives, Guru Gobind Singh acted like a saint and Aurangzeb became a villain according to Sikhism or Hindu history.

Something must have triggered Aurangzeb to commit such acts or the family he was born in was responsible for his actions. Once you reach a certain crunch point, any villain or saint can transform into either character. If you can hold on to your nerve, you are a saint; if not, you become a villain. Sadly, so many saints suffer at the hands of villains and millions of people die every year without seeing or receiving any justice.

'Will there be one? People are scared for their lives and hiding but culprits are roaming free and laughing. In English, there is a saying that every dog has his day. I know so many people who died but never had their day. This saddens me sometimes. I was given the wrong advice by my guru many times. I listened in good faith and followed instructions; due to that, I have suffered and am suffering today. Many times, I wonder why.

During my training in master-ship, I wished the floodgates of Spirit should open so I could pass the message of God. I noticed that the spiritual Master entirely controlled me not to commit any mistakes but those who purposely did wrong against me were not. Now I have come to a certain age where I wish no spiritual floodgates would open for me. God is the creator of the whole creation and Kal is also part of God. With experience, I can say God is the creator and experiencer.

So, who is the Villain or Saint?

WEAK AURA & BLACK MAGIC

Most of the time, we are responsible for our suffering. Although we believe we are the followers of Spirit, at the same time, we are following some other practices too. As the saying goes, you cannot sail in two boats simultaneously. These other practices will become your failure point. Although you are trying to achieve something (extra knowledge), it provides resistance to the Holy Spirit, bringing so many difficulties to the Seeker of truth. Your spiritual aura becomes weak. Many entities, black magic or someone's anger, can easily penetrate this weak aura.

A. Take a look at this golden ball which provides Spiritual shield

B. This spiritual shield with holes, it provides less protection.

How to Remove This Entity

Once aware that someone else is living within this aura, you will face many difficulties in life. It could be health or wealth problems or this spirit can stir anger within to create negative scenes in your family where everyone is disturbed. It is about time to take action to remove this negative entity from your aura and lead life back to normal. I will give you a straightforward meditation exercise with a self-explanatory sketch.

You may sit in a tailor fashion or any other acceptable position to meditate. Take ten deep breaths to relax. Repeat this breathing procedure until you feel fully relaxed. Begin to chant your holy word or Haiome. Continue chanting until you feel the sensation of spiritual vibrations and a warm feeling within your forehead. When you are ready, create a spiritual circle or shield around yourself, as shown in the diagram.

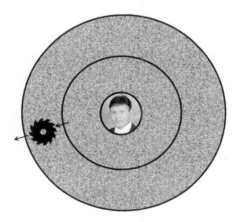

Next, create an image of a disturbing entity in your life. See in your vision that it is moving out of your spiritual shield or aura, as demonstrated during our practical workshops. Repeat this a few times until you feel success.

DISCOVER YOURSELF

We have forgotten how to discover ourselves. We are more interested in the truth discovered by someone else; the most significant finding is sitting within us. Bible, Qur'an, Bhagwat Gita or any other is not your exploration of truth. You are abiding by someone else's explored truth. If you feel about leaving your religion and finding out what other teachings are saying, something within is asking you to move on; there is more to learn.

This applies to any Seeker who wants to explore spiritual truth for themselves. There is someone who knows better and you are searching for this spiritual Master. We do this silently or openly declare, 'I am off to follow this Master to find the truth more thoroughly.' Your religious family will be stopping you from doing this. They have many explanations for this. You should never follow a living Master; they are all misleading or will rob you of your money.

They recommend following a book written by someone a few thousand years ago. 'Can anyone tell me since when can a book be your living Master? You can believe what you like; that is your free will. They don't want you to leave their **circle**. It is their fear that you may discover the truth. I have done my exploration, so I am writing something new every day. It is all coming from within. These people have gone rusty and can hardly think beyond their doorsteps.

Since I mentioned this word **circle,** I remember my own experience when I was a child. This kind of experience occurs quite often in village life. This is an example and I have no intention of ridiculing any person or religion. You may know female snakes produce at least one hundred eggs in one go. Once I witnessed when they were hatching. The female snake formed a coil around all eggs during this process; the baby snakes began to appear in no time.

They were so many and were desperate to get out of the coil due to a lack of space. Many circled within the coil of the mother. The mother began to eat them; only a few managed to escape from this circle. This was early learning and a turning point in my life. View this life with an open mind; you can learn abundant knowledge. All these priests are not only concerned with their followers but they intervene with other religious followers as well.

It is called a forced religious conversion. This is the biggest sin anyone can commit. Those who accept conversion are from poor backgrounds and these priests take advantage of this and try to meet their physical needs, such as food and shelter. Unknowingly, these poor people walk into a trap. When realisation comes, it is too late and beyond their control. Exploring within on a spiritual basis was unknown.

Michael was second in command 'Manager' where I used to work, with at least four hundred people working under him. We were pretty close friends and one day; he came to see me for advice. He said, Mr Gill, I am leaving this job in a few days. 'Can you advise me if I am making the right decision? I asked why. He was under thirty years of age and his future was ahead of him. He said, I want to explore this world and I am arranging for a world tour. I advised him not to do it.

You are so young and have a highly paid and respectful job. Michael said; I have made up my mind. This is the right time and age to explore this world. Later, I may not be able to do what I can do now. After a few days, he packed up his bags and explored the world to his maximum ability. He had enough cash but I asked, 'If you run out of money, what will you do? He replied; I don't mind washing dirty plates in some restaurant. This exploration is significant to me. That is what I call determination. 'How can this person fail in his life?

When I was so dedicated to discovering the truth, I had been ridiculed or insulted a few times by my own near and dear ones but I never cared. I did discover what I went out to discover but at the same time, those wounds of insults I received are still evident. This is why I want to be alone and live in my self-explored world. All these relations we value most are nothing but pain to carry on our shoulders.

I discover something every day. Spirit asked me today to sit down and write. I took the whole dictation in twenty minutes on a piece of paper. I know all these things but Spirit dictates me to write in such a manner and I am amazed. Many people believe only in watching their religious programs on TV and not the others and they recommend the same to others.

In a sense, maybe they are correct but at the same time, they fear that you may discover something which they don't want you to discover. I love all comedy programs and humour in life is very important. I used to watch *Father Ted* and which was a Christian-based comedy program. Father Ted was in the lead role and Father Dougal was in the side role. Jack was the old father who always sat in his chair with a bottle (alcohol) in his hand.

It did not matter to him what subject was being discussed whenever they asked his opinion on what had been said; he always replied with one word: 'Drink.' That was part of the humour in this program. Like Father Jack, most people have only a few words on their minds; drink, food or sleep. This way of life, you cannot progress physically or spiritually. When most significant truth is waiting for you to discover.

I discovered many things while listening to many people from all walks of life. British mice live in the underground burrow system. You cannot catch mice by sitting outside the burrow. You have to put your hand in the mice's den. You may catch it or the mice may bite your hand but this is the only way to find the truth if mice live in this burrow. This is only an example, don't practice it.

Truth comes to me every day; I often fail to acknowledge it when I don't bother to write it. 'Ask yourself what have you explored so far? The answer will be almost nothing. Most people's exploration finishes with eating spicy foods in some restaurants. You only managed to explore the mind's faculty known as taste. In your whole life, your exploration comes to one percent.

My background is Sikhism; once I was talking to another Sikh friend about God. I thought he was interested in knowing the truth, so I offered him one book to read. After a few days, he returned the book. I asked him if he had read it. He said yes. I said excellent and left him there to ask if he was interested to know more. After a short while, I learned that he never read it because it was written by an American.

He took it only to make fun of me. I never contacted him in the future. He lived an alcoholic life in his later years and died from many organ failures, so he wasted his life doing nothing. He can never learn what I discovered in this life. Ignorance is the biggest obstacle in life and he was so close to knowing the truth. I learned something while reading a book written by a red Indian saint and a few others.

All these people give you some idea of how to search for truth. If you imitate the life of some known saint, you can discover half the truth. When you discover the whole truth, you are a saint. Too much complaining about life at present is the biggest obstacle to discovering any truth at all. All these Christians knocking on your door on Sunday are not there to show you the truth of God. They want you to join them. Truth is never discovered in groups; it is a personal discovery.

It is never too late to discover yourself. Alexander the Great set his goal to conquer the whole world. Columbus was an Italian explorer and navigator who made four voyages and discovered America. New Zealander Edmund Hillary and Sherpa Tenzing were the first two to climb Mount Everest. At the end of this chapter, you may ask yourself, 'What did I discover? You are right; nothing. 'Do you know why? Because you have never managed to set foot outside your doorstep.

I have given some examples to discover yourself. I leave it in your hands. I cannot eat or drink on your behalf, nor can I find out the truth on your behalf.

My discovery is my own. You have to discover yourself.

DOOMSDAY OR DOOMED

The word *doomsday* is very frightening; we expect something big to happen by nature in this world. That is true but it does not happen quite often. Doomsday is a time of crisis and on a small scale, it takes place in everyone's life. Some are saying Kryptonians or a secret society of super-villains are going to come. Don't you think we already have many super-villains in this world?

A reasonably big doomsday is expected around 2029/30 but I am not certain of the exact date. During the BC era, God instructed Noah to build an ark because heavy floods were coming to destroy that area. Recently, a tsunami came on 2 December 2004, hitting Thailand and nearby islands and approximately 229,000 people lost their lives. These are natural disasters that don't happen quite often.

We witnessed many wars and civil wars in Afghanistan, Iraq, Syria and more within the last twenty years. They all are man-created doomsdays and people are suffering because of that. Nowadays, you cannot forecast which country will create a new doomsday for its people or the rest of the world. At present, a few countries are doomed by nature or by their group karma. Governments fail to provide water, food or shelter to their citizens and ask for help from well-off countries.

The starving or hungry person will not wait for any doomsday; he is doomed now. Similarly, many of us feel doomed, not knowing why. We want to move on in our lives but we fail every time for many reasons, even though we do nothing wrong. Our bad karma is holding us down or some psychic attack. Despite your good efforts and achievements, you cannot feel glorified.

You want to laugh but there is little pain behind this, so you cannot laugh openly. We admire royal families or super-rich people because of their wealth and status. 'Do you know they are the most doomed people on earth because they have lost their free will? They cannot leave their palaces without taking precautions and they cannot utter any rude words or make silly statements because they are answerable to every word.

They cannot live everyday lives because of their palaces. It is the biggest stage of acting and you have to stay in character. The Oscar awards are too small for their acting skills. It is their good karma to achieve all this limelight and at the same time, it demands full payment in many ways. Any middle-class family can lead a happier life than the royals. Royals and wealthy families are doomed to stay within the walls of big palaces and they are the prisoners of being rich and famous.

'Do you know that many politicians are better actors than movie stars? They can deliver dialogues and command the language. It is the same with many known celebrities becoming rich and famous overnight and it is equal to depression. Many become alcoholics or use heavy drugs. A name and fame can be lost in no time; they are forced to lead doomed, depressed lives, leading to suicides in many cases.

Several natural doomsdays are coming in the future and at that time, the power of Shiva the destroyer comes into action. I will give you some historical facts and figures about famous people who created a doomsday for their people and the rest of the world. All these people are responsible for the deaths of millions of civilians or military personnel during the last century to maintain their power.

Name	Ruled	Death Toll
Enver Pasha of Turkey	1913–18	1.1 million
Kim Sung of North Korea	1948–94	1.6 million
Ho Chi Minh of North Vietnam	1945–69	1.7 million
Pol Pot of Columbia	1975–79	1.7 million
Saddam Hussein of Iraq	1969–2003	2 million
Yahya Khan of Pakistan	1969–71	2 million
Hideki Tojo of Japan	1941–44	4 million
Vladimir Lenin of Russia	1917–24	6 million
Hirohito of Japan	1926–89	6 million
Chiang Kai-Shek of China	1928–49	10 million
Adolf Hitler of Germany	1934–45	20 million
Joseph Stalin of Russia	1941–53	23 million
Mao Zedong of China	1943–76	42.5 million

All these facts and figures are available on Google. We can mention so many other names; Mr Idi Amin of Uganda, Colonel Gaddafi of Libya, American presidents involved in many countries. There is no end to this list. Natural disasters should not worry you as much because nature always gives some warning before it happens. You should watch out for our world politicians; you never know who will create doomsday and when.

You may not know some countries have focused their nuclear missiles with a fixed range and target to destroy major cities of this world. If any person in charge in these places loses one's temper or gets depressed, it could be due to personal problems and can trigger the buttons. It is the disbelief of religious people that one day God will destroy this world. I can assure you that we humans will make sure this world is destroyed one day.

ETERNAL YOUTH

I am sure this is one of the favourite subjects of everyone in this world. We admire ourselves every morning by standing in front of the mirror. Some people do this all day, especially those in the film industry or modelling. People spend a fortune on beauty products or plastic surgery. 'Do you know all these practices push forward to age quicker and many plastic surgeries have gone wrong? You have lost a little bit of youth you had. This is why some people believe in ageing gracefully.

Many religions stress to remember; you will die one day. They mean you should not commit any bad karma because, after death, you will face the king of the dead, where all your wrong-doings will be counted for. Instead, people take it the other way; that you will die one day. These thoughts bring fear within and this fear becomes the killer of your youth.

One of the best-known practices is to do regular physical exercise and pay attention to your diet. This way, you can feel better and stay healthy most of your life but age and family genes play their part too. Despite all your efforts, wrinkles begin to appear and hair turns grey; hair loss is common. I knew one saint named Baba Sadhu Singh; I did mention his name in my book *The Will of God*. He knew me since I was a child when I was about fourteen and he was fifty-two years old. At that time, all his beard was white or grey.

The last time I saw him, in 2006, he was ninety-one years old. To my surprise, most of his beard had turned back to its original black colour. I have the photos to prove the before and after. During this meeting, we discussed it and the conclusion was that as a saint, he has been in meditation most of his life. I noticed that he lost some body weight but he remarked that he hardly felt the need for physical food.

I have written that in Agam-Des, where 'Yabal Sakabi' is in charge of this spiritual city, all the people working for him are called God-eaters (spiritual energy). It is the atmosphere within this spiritual city and the work they do. It is all related to Spirit. When doing this kind of work, you are dwelling in Spirit. Spirit becomes your food intake instead of physical food; with this spiritual food, you do not age.

For example, if you are a youth of twenty-five years, you will remain the same forever as long as you are part of this spiritual city. No one wants to leave but everyone is not welcome to stay or join. Many visitors come to receive teachings and they leave at the end of the discourse. All these visitors are also saints or soul travellers. This spiritual city is in the remote Hindu-Kush Mountains, near the border of Afghanistan and Kashmir.

These mountains are the origin of many rivers and one of them is the Jhelum. At the headwaters of this river, there is a spring of pure water known as Nirmala-Charan, the fountain of youth or the waters of immortality. After drinking this water, any person can become immortal. Very few are aware of this and it is their secret to stay young forever for those saints based there. This spot is not very easy to find and is guarded by the Spirit.

Alexander the Great was born in Pella, Greece, in 356 BC and died very young at thirty-two years in Babylon on 10 June 323 BC. The cause of his death is still unknown. After conquering the empire of Persia, Alexander entered these mountains to wage war against King Porus of Punjab, Pakistan. When Alexander reached this point, a spiritual saint appeared with Nirmala-Charan and offered for Alexander to drink it.

This saint could see the future and the killing of so many innocent people. If Alexander drank this water, his war intentions would change and he would become a spiritual at heart. Alexander was a king and did not trust this offering, taking it as some kind of deception. As he drew his sword to strike this saint, the man disappeared into thin air. The battle took place between King Porus and Alexander. Alexander won the war but became friends with King Porus.

He desired to conquer the whole world but he returned to the West from there. This battle is known as the Battle of River Jhelum. I think it was his destiny to reach India and fight. I also mentioned another saint, Baba Harnam Singh, in our Bhagty-Marg chapter in *The Way of God*. Once, he decided to sit for lengthy meditation, which was at least one year in one go, without getting up to achieve any spiritual success.

The question is, who was looking after his body and food? It was Spirit. When you are so dedicated, you become part of God's spiritual scheme or become a God-eater. You do not consume any physical food but Spirit within will provide for all relevant needs. You can live without any intake of physical food or drinking water. There is a pure spiritual fountain within. I do not have to prove this to anyone but those very close to me know that I have hardly eaten for the last four to five years.

Also, I did not drink clear water all my life. Sometimes I wonder why people drink so much water and they say you cannot live without it. Yes, maybe. I do drink some tea or juice but I never experienced what thirst or hunger is. All these foods and liquids are necessary to eat or drink. At the same time, people age, so this cannot be the perfect food for us. Up to some extent, I have access to this spiritual food and one time, I thought of staying young forever like Rebazar and many others.

It took me a few years to understand not doing it, so I changed my mind. I felt that it is good to stay young and achieve longevity but after many years, when all known people pass away and new generations appear, you become unknown to them and a stranger to everyone. Longevity is more a phenomenon to be created than pleasure. Then you will lose your interest in living any more physically unless you have been given some spiritual task like many other saints.

There are ways and means of maintaining eternal youth forever but you have to adopt spiritual living practices or you can live for a very long life as you have become a spiritual saint. Then you can also leave your body at will and move into the eternal world of the living. Eternal youth is only possible once you move out of mortal living. We can do so much but we are so attached to this world that we forget to explore our true abilities. You can do whatever you imagine because it already exists; otherwise, you cannot imagine it.

May you live forever

IMPORTANCE OF LIVING

The physical embodiment is essential to acknowledge any achievement in this world. Otherwise, it does not exist as far as this world is concerned. I know there are so many spiritual beings working in invisible forms to keep the balance of all universes but no one knows that it is taking place. They need to do this but it is not acknowledged worldwide. All these presidents and prime ministers think that they are running this world. On the contrary, these unknown spiritual beings are sorting out the destruction created by our world's political conflicts.

These spiritual corrections are never acknowledged because they cannot be recorded anywhere. It is why the importance of living is necessary if you want to make your mark in this world. How important is it to make your mark in this world? As far as I am concerned, not at all. Most extraordinary people don't want their work to be acknowledged because whatever they are doing is for them to know only. People around you notice what you do and they talk about it because they are learning from what you provide.

Otherwise, this extraordinary knowledge is beyond their reach. This way, you have left your mark in this world through these people. It is essential to do something worthwhile; otherwise, thousands of children are born every day and thousands of people die every day but no one knows who they are. Due to many known or unknown reasons,

I am here and doing my spiritual endeavours but I do not wish to be acknowledged.

I cannot help writing what I know. God has given me the gift of spiritual knowledge and in that sense, I feel my duty that others should know so they can benefit too. I do not approach anyone for this but whoever somehow comes my way to learn what I know. I tell them it is their free will to apply spiritual principles in their lives. This way, what you know automatically becomes your mark in this world. Despite all this, I wish that people should not know who I was at the end of my life span.

But while I am still living, I am learning too. That is a plus point for my soul because any journey made into the physical world is never wasted. Each journey is important because we learn something and it is recorded in the files what takes place. The lower worlds are our training ground and the soul has left its true home in the spiritual worlds to learn. It is similar to how we leave our homes and walk to school every day for this purpose. All these academic qualifications are achieved only by leaving home. It is not possible to achieve the same by sitting at home.

Lead your life as directed by God.

MY SPIRITUAL JOURNEY
BY SEEKER

The spiritual Master always says, 'Truth is never denied if the Seeker is ready.' I said many times; if the Seeker is serious on this spiritual path and is willing to listen and follow instructions from the Master, then five years is far too long. The Seeker has been our member for just three years and has explored the kingdom of God up to the God-realisation position. The whole experience took place in one night on 15 May 2018.

The Seeker took the teachings very seriously from day one and had lots of good karma from previous lives. There are eleven experiences in total. The Seeker had many other very uplifting spiritual experiences within the last three years. Ten experiences took place in one night and one prior experience relating to this realisation is shown in advance. The Seeker is physically awake at the beginning and end of each experience, to acknowledge what has taken place.

Each time the Seeker noted the time. During these experiences, the Master and Spirit take over the Seeker's spiritual journey. The Seeker has seen so much but we have tried to use a minimum of words. I am sure this experience will encourage so many Seekers who want to see a glimpse of God's world. The following are the Seeker's own words.

First Experience: Spiritual Masters, 11 p.m.

I was sitting with precious, my dog because she was not feeling well. I stroked her back and said Satnam Ji (lord of the soul plane). Then suddenly, an experience opened up and all world-famous Spiritual Masters or Gurus began to appear before me one by one. It was a small screen before my eyes and each Master appeared not as in a still photograph but as if they were alive. Once I was satisfied with a glimpse of any Master, then the next Master would appear on the same screen.

Darshan means the glimpse of a holy man. This Darshan of Masters begins with Guru Nanak Dev of Sikhism, followed by nine other gurus. These were the ten gurus of Sikhism and followed by Baba Nand Singh and Isher Singh of Nanak Sar and Baba Isher Singh Ji of Rarhe-wale. They were followed by all gurus of Hinduism, such as Sri Ram, Sri Krishna, Shiv Ji, Parvati and Mahatma Buddha.

Then Sri Paul Ji, Dapren, Shams Mohd of Tabriji, Rebazar Tarz, Fubbi Kants, Yam-Raj, Yam-Dutes, Jesus Christ, Mohammad and so many more were introduced by Sher Ji. I was told the name of each Master. I can clearly state I had the privilege of seeing all world spiritual Masters who ever existed. Once this Darshan ended, I returned to my normal state again, thanked Master Sher Ji and said, 'Shukria' thank you, Satnam Ji.' Another experience opened up. 'Shukria means thank you.'

Second Experience: My Past Lives

Sher Ji asked me if I wanted to see my past lives. I was so glad to hear this and instantly, I said '**Yes.**' In most of my past lives,

I was a very beautiful and glamorous woman in different countries. I was a black woman who was so beautiful and later, I was an English lady sitting in horse-driven carts. Next, I saw that I was part of the Indian royal family (Shahi-Parivar), princess of one of the Riyasat means '**State.**'

I saw myself as female or in female costumes in most of my past lives. I asked Sher Ji, 'Have I been female all the time?

He replied, **No.** First, you will see all important female-based past lives. Then I will show you your male-based past lives. After this conversation, I was shown all my past lives as a male. I saw myself living in different countries and holding different statuses in these lives, whether rich or poor and living in a hut. I lived in jungles and was also part of different religions according to the country I was living in.

All souls go through this process of male or female forms while incarnated on the physical plane. In one of them, I was responsible for looking after the final resting place of Shiv Ji in India. After learning and seeing so much, I asked Sher Ji to pause for a little while so I could write down what I had seen so far. Otherwise, I would not be able to remember everything. Sher Ji replied in Punjabi, 'Kaun Kambakhat Kehnda Hai ke Yaad Rakh? Who fool asks you to remember all?

What you saw so far is your past and gone. Sher Ji added, 'Look ahead and carry on with your spiritual life.' If you require any important information in the future from your past lives, it will be revealed to you in flashbacks. Looking at Sher Ji, I said, I am very grateful. Then I said, 'Shukria' thank you to Satnam Ji,' and suddenly, another experience began. I remember saying to Sher Ji, 'What you have shown

me so far is more than enough for tonight. Now it is too late
and I want to go to sleep.'

Sher Ji told me off and said in Punjabi, 'Tu bahut Boldi hai,
Tenu chup rehan di lorh hai. "You speak too much; you
need to stay in silence" He also said to me, 'Stay in silence
for a few days so that I can stay in balance after seeing and
knowing so much.' Then Sher Ji added; Today, I want to
give you lots of spiritual teachings, so do not interrupt me.

Third Experience: Journey

In this experience, Sher Ji and I walked along the farmlands
where wheat was grown. I began to walk on top of the bank
of the small water Canal (Khaal) and I was slipping from this
tapered bank time after time. I asked Sher Ji if I could walk
in the middle of the canal, which was used to provide water
to boost the growth of wheat. This canal was empty or dry
at that time. He said; Yes but stay in gunnia (balance).

It was a very long walk and suddenly water began to flow in
this canal. Gradually the water level rises. As we walked
ahead, I saw lots of dry leaves and dry grass being collected
and a whirlpool appeared. I was standing in front of that
whirlpool and suddenly water came with lots of pressure.
I fell on my back. My feet were pointing at the whirlpool
and the next minute; I felt that I had been pushed into the
whirlpool.

I was sliding along the flow of high-speed water and there
were lots of curves in this canal. I faced the challenge at
every bend and my body often did somersaults. The water
was so cold and clean that it seemed ice had just melted.
After enjoying my long ride above the water, my body was

thrown into the melted golden ocean. My eyes opened and
I said, 'Shukria' thank you, Satnam Ji.' My next experience
opened up.

Fourth Experience: Karma-less

I remember saying to myself; I won't say, 'Shukria, thank
you, Satnam Ji,' because every time I mention these words,
the experience begins. I was trying to avoid any future
experiences because I was so happy with what I had seen. As
soon as I mentioned the words again for not saying, 'Shukria,
Satnam Ji,' I felt a sharp pain. I felt a sharp needle being
poked in my left shoulder and I said again, 'I am not going to
say Shukria.'

Another sharp needle was poked in my left arm and I said,
'You can sew me with needles if you want to, Satnam Ji.
After that, my whole body was poked with needles from all
directions. I heard Sher Ji saying, 'One more needle to go on
top of your head. That is when the whole process will finish.'
Then I heard a very loud voice and someone called Sher Ji by
another name, **Avtar,** a spiritual name. I saw a very big giant
coming down from a very high place. He had a body like any
body builder; big muscles, a wide chest and a bald head.

As he came down, Sher Ji had the last needle to poke in my
head and as soon as that needle went in my head, the big
giant fell on top of me and entered my body. Then Sher Ji
entered and disappeared into my body too. I heard that the
big giant asked Sher Ji if he could remove all the needles
from my body. Then Sher Ji removed most of the needles
and when Sher Ji began to remove needles from my left arm,
I stopped him by saying, 'Please leave these few needles in
my left arm so that I will stay connected with you.'

Then I woke up and said, 'Shukria, thank you, Satnam Ji.' This big giant was Satnam Ji and poking needles in the body symbolises defusing karma. Only karma-less people can enter the soul plane, so Sher Ji was preparing my journey into the purely spiritual planes. Leaving a few needles in my arm is a symbol to indicate that my karma account is still open in this world till the end of my present life span.

Fifth Experience: Crossing the Lower Plane

In this experience, as soon as I said, 'Satnam Ji.' I was sitting on the edge of my bed **awake** and saw Sher Ji walk into my room. I looked into his eyes, which were shining like spotlights. He had long, curly hair and did not utter a single word to me. He kept looking at me and in the next minute, I could see that Sher Ji had turned into a big, shining star and I was a star too. The big, bright star was going up and up very fast and I followed the big star.

We, like stars, were going through so many different clouds, Green, Pink, Orange, Blue and Purple clouds. All colours are a symbol of crossing each lower plane. We approached Golden clouds and then Sher Ji said to me, come quick and fast; we need to crossover to the other side before the door closes. I could see there was a little pathway to follow and a very narrow door. I saw the big shining star go through and asked me to be very quick as the door was about to close.

I tried my best to go as fast as I could. I was in the middle of crossing that slim door and it was closing. I got stuck in that door. It was so tight that I tried to pull myself out and finally, I managed to pull myself as a star. After that, I looked like a long, slim, shining star with a tail. My tail got stuck in that tight door, which was very painful. With pain,

I woke up physically. Sher Ji said, 'We have to try some other time again.'

My little tail stuck in that door is a symbol of indicating that a little more preparation is required or it was reluctance on my part because I had already seen beyond my expectations.

Sixth Experience: Final Crossover

I was trying to sleep after having so many experiences in one night. I saw Sher Ji again in my room and I remember saying to him, 'You are back again, Sher Veer Ji; means Brother' I cannot take any more teachings tonight because I am tired. How will I remember all this? You don't even allow me time to write in my book.

Sher Ji said in Punjabi, 'Kaun Kambakhat Kehnda Ke Yaad Rakh Sabh Kush. 'Who fool asks you to remember everything? Everything will go in your subconscious mind and each page will come out when required. (Harek panna jaddo jaroorat paie) In Punjabi. He told me off because I spoke a lot and Sher Ji said, 'I will make your stay in an Aeroplane and strike you off on the way to Heathrow Airport because you are speaking too much.'

The next minute, I found myself turned into a model of an Aeroplane. Sher Ji told me; Go into the inner worlds and on the other side of the soul plane. I obeyed and began my journey but the Aeroplane was so heavy and had no flexibility. I found it very difficult to move that Aeroplane through slim streets within high golden buildings. Then I told Sher Ji that I wanted to change my plans to reach the other side. Sher Ji said, 'Yes, as you wish.'

I thanked Sher Ji and said; I will try again with my **guardian angel** but not now, some other time. Sher Ji said, 'It is up to you how quickly you want to do so. The longer you wait, the longer you have to bear the pain in your tail.' OK, Sher Ji, we will go there very soon. I tried to sleep and then Precious, my dog, woke me up because she wanted to go outside as usual. I got out of my bed to take Precious to the back garden.

Seventh Experience: 3.50 a.m.

I took Precious out. It was very regular for her to wake me up at this time, between 3.30 and 4 a.m. After some time, I called Precious to come back indoors. She was coming towards the kitchen door from the other end of the garden and as she reached the halfway point, I heard someone say to her, 'Rukk; means stop.' Precious stopped and turned her face back and she kept watching someone for a long time. I called her again to come back indoors. She came back and I heard the words, 'See you on the other side.'

Sher Ji crept inside the house and I said to him, 'I can see you are back again.'

He told me off and screamed at me, 'Mai tere aaj Thappar Marna Hai.' I am going to slap you today.

I said to Sher Ji; First, you tell me who gave you the right to tell me off like this?

He replied; You have given me this right. 'Do you remember the day you came for your initiation and I asked you to bring five fruits? During initiation, I explained that these five fruits symbolise submitting your five bodies physical, astral, causal, mental and soul, to the Spirit. Now I am in you and you are in me. I bent down to him and touched his feet in respect for the first time. I went upstairs to my room and heard Sher Ji saying to me, 'Try again with the **guardian angel** to go to the other end.'

I said, ok, Sher Ji.

Eighth Experience: Success

The **guardian angel** said; Shall we go? I said, 'Yes, let us go.'

The angel and I were flying so high in the sky and saw many beautiful cities and buildings of purple colour and beautiful gardens with purple flowers and many more. Purple colour is a symbol of being in an Etheric or Sub-Conscious Plane. After a beautiful purple city, we went to the city of gold and again there were beautiful high buildings. The angel was flying so high and so fast.

Then suddenly, the guardian angel began to fly even faster and asked me to hold on to her tightly. The angel said; We have to reach the other end before the door shuts. The door was about to close. Then the angel kept flying like a big bird through narrow streets and high buildings. We saw a little door and the angel and I both smiled as she said, 'We are nearly there.' We could see the door, which we had to cross to go to the other side of the soul plane.

The angel said, 'Hold on to me very tight. We both wanted to reach the other side and angel jumped through that door as it was closing. We managed to go through that door and the angel said, 'We have done it.' Upon reaching the other side of that door, I saw a big gold brick in front of my eyes, sitting on the tip of my nose. This gold brick was shining so brightly that I could not see anything; I asked Sher Ji, 'What is this?

He said, 'Keep on walking.' I obeyed him and continued.

That gold brick begins to move slowly to my right side. I saw a very muddy, slim walkway that was very curly; I kept walking, which turned into a straight path with golden bricks laid in a beautiful design. Then I noticed a milestone on my left and it was made of gold. As I kept walking, a few more milestones came. On the last one, there were some numbers, 41788, indicating many more milestones to my final destination.

Far away, I saw another huge white milestone as our journey continued. On this milestone, letters were written vertically. Vertical is also a symbol of travelling to the higher planes. I tried to read but it was difficult because we moved along. I tried once more and read only the first three letters; ANA ... Anami-Lok is the tenth spiritual plane. If we add up all these numbers or milestones, it is $4 + 1 + 7 + 8 + 8 = 28$.

If we further add up, then 28 is $2 + 8 = 10$, which also indicates your final destination is Anami-Lok. It is unbelievable how accurate Spirit is when showing all these symbols. All we need is a little effort to unveil the mystery of the symbol and understand the actual meaning of the experience taking place. As the experience continued, anything in our vision was pure white or silver. White or silver are symbols of higher planes above the soul plane.

Soul Plane is gold - Alakh is light gold – Alaya - is a fading gold. Hakikat, Agam and Anami-lok are pure white or silver. The destination to Anami-Lok was reached. As soon as this experience finished, I woke up and said, 'Shukria, thank you, Satnam Ji,' and another experience opened.

It seems that '**Shukria, Satnam Ji**' is my
magic word to the secret world.

Ninth Experience: Celebration

The night of 15 May was my blessed night because I had so many experiences. Again, Sher Ji came into my room with another seven Masters. I was so glad and did not know what to say or do. Then we all ate Besan Ladoos (an Indian sweet) to celebrate my spiritual journey. As the Masters were leaving, they blessed me too. Sher Ji said, 'Now I am going as well.'

I asked him, 'Is there any message for me?

He said; You are a naked soul. 'He opened my front door to leave.' Upon asking, Sher Ji explained to me, 'Naked soul means you are karma-less; otherwise, you would not be travelling this far.' I thanked God and said, 'Shukria, Satnam Ji,' and instantly, another experience started.

Tenth Experience: Future

Sher Ji came back and said; I will show you your future.

I said, 'What did you say, Sher Ji? He said you heard me correct. He showed me my future and told me, 'Now write your future in your own words, in the shape of a manuscript (book). You will not remember what you have just seen but once any critical situation or happening occurs in your life, you will see the same situation in flashbacks. At the end of this experience, I came back to my normal senses, noting the time; 7 a.m.

During the second experience, I saw my past lives and in this experience, I have seen the future. To know your future is promising but at the same time, learning a few situations upfront could be disturbing because they may not be in your favour. This is the story of each individual and on that basis, God draws a curtain over our past lives and future.

Sher Ji told me that in the future, when any critical situation takes place, there and then I will get the flashback and knowingness will come to indicate that this was shown to me earlier. Since that day, a few important situations have occurred in my life and instantly, I saw the flashback of acknowledging the information received earlier. This is exactly what happened in the history of Hinduism.

Saint Valmiki wrote Ramayana before the story of Ramayana was completed in real life. So, this chapter will be my Ramayana and it is going to reveal my future because it will unfold or take shape in my life. At the beginning or end of each experience, I was fully awake physically and noted the time on the clock. During the experiences, it was spiritual Master Sher Ji teaching and my soul was learning.

I am blessed by Spirit, Sher Ji and Satnam Ji. According to my eighth experience, we added up all numbers 41788 and the answer came as 10, which was our symbol for Anami-Lok. If we add up 10 in the same manner (1 + 0), the answer is 1. There is only one God, so I am blessed by God too. May the blessings be.

Mrs Arvind Kuner; 15 May 2018

To the Seeker; you have seen the truth. Now you are the Master of your universe.

Sher Gill

MY UNIVERSE

It is a misfortune for this world; most countries and religions are divided so badly they aim to over-powerful others. Some are silent, while most declare enemies of this or that country or religion openly. Each is power-hungry and tries to outsmart the others. They all want to dominate, 'But to whom? To the whole world, in effect, they are deceiving themselves. 'What is this wholeness?

They will never understand; we are incomplete without the others, not by power but without their love. It is the love of this universe that makes you complete. There is a million miles of a gap between us as humans. 'Do you know why? Religions are the leading cause. We believe our religions lead us to God but they only add oil to the fire. These religious scholars are so busy, they have forgotten God and accepted politics as their goal.

Most politicians waste energy on how to complete several terms. You can conclude, 'Are they interested in you or keen on self-service? It is not limited to them only; they pass over the power to future generations. I can name a few of these families in India and Pakistan. Their present generations cannot lead their nations but their entire force is used to make them the forefront faces of their countries.

All these ministers and presidents promise to serve their countries but most of their energy is used to overload their bank accounts. 'What can these nations gain under this kind of leadership? It is disgraceful and unfortunate for these countries. That is why these countries are called Third World countries. God created this world to look like heaven and all humans are created equal and very close to its heart. But these power-hungry people call themselves kings, queens and ministers, while most of the public is called labourers, enslaved people or low caste.

In the eyes of God, there is no caste, no rich or poor, just princes and princesses of God and heirs to the throne. Religious saints and astrologers threaten this world many times that God will destroy this world on a particular day. 'None of their forecasts have come true; do you know why? They are all fake gurus and misusing people's invested trust. All major religions of this world are the backbone of politics.

Where is God? Who is God? It is all forgotten. All nuclear-minded countries will destroy this world but not God. There is no value for human life; history repeats itself every few years. All-powerful people receive some prophecy by some live oracles, saints or astrologers, to the effect that they were born to rule this world. Once this belief imprints in their minds, all their actions are naturally driven to execute this prophecy; the cost or loss is never considered.

These oracles, saints and astrologers are responsible for many destructions. This was part of Alexander's belief and many others. In the early days, Alexander the Great was one man who wished to rule this world. After the assassination of his father, King Phillip, it is believed he was the son of Zeus, who was considered the ruler of Olympian gods in Greece.

His mother claimed, one day before her wedding, that the spiritual light of Zeus struck into her womb and she felt the pregnancy. Alexander killed every man who stood in his path of power. His journey begins from Macedonia to the Persian Empire and finally to India. During his invasion trip to other countries, at least one million people died. This was a very high number of deaths considering the population.

In World War I, the total number of casualties accounted for was 41 million, comprising 11 million military deaths, 7 million civilians died and 23 million wounded.

In World War II, the total number of casualties is unknown but over 60 million people died. About 20 million military personnel and 40 million civilians were killed due to bombing, massacres, starvation, diseases and deliberate genocide. At least 1.3 million British military personnel died in this war.

During the Napoleonic war, the battlefields toured Egypt, Belgium, Holland, Italy, Austria, Germany, Poland, Spain and most of Europe. 'Can you imagine the number of people dead or wounded? If you go through world history and see how many major wars or conflicts took place and how many people died, you will be speechless. 'Are we still blaming God for this?

Some countries are ready to repeat this history if they get the opportunity. 'Can someone tell me what God has to do with this? These fake saints and astrologers are pulling some cheap stunts by saying God will destroy this or that. God is the creator of all universes, not the destroyer. Humans are always responsible for their destruction for several reasons.

The whole world is divided. Forget about the nations with the help of Kal; there is a mini Government within each family. There is no evidence of God's love and domination over others are more important. I wish everyone could think, act or believe as I do. I am part of the whole universe. I do not believe in any religion or any particular country. The entire universe is mine and destruction can only stop when we act as one.

When you are a universal being, it is so satisfying and peaceful. Being part of only one country or religion is irritating because you have no tolerance for others. We are pilgrims here to do spiritual learning and die naturally. Regarding the land you claimed to be yours in deed-papers, someone else's name will appear on the papers after your death. It is the same land and will remain the same; only the ownership names change and nothing you can do about it.

This world is created as a whole. This whole land is joined together as one piece on the surface or under the sea. All five oceans are one too. All these religions are man-made. It is the weakness of humans to follow one for many purposes, create self-identity and socialise with each other. All religions have become part of politics, so they fail to give spiritual succour to their followers. To socialise is good for occupying the mind; it is also responsible for self-created problems.

People are more interested in sorting out self-created problems than God. This is why God is beyond their reach. One day, they will realise that God is waiting for them with open arms.

May the truth be yours.

SILENT LEGENDS

There are thousands of silent legends; we cannot mention their names because they always remain anonymous. We cannot write much on this subject for the same reason. Many people live in remote places or make sure their identities remain hidden. You will notice that most of them are shy. They are not working for name or fame. Many people don't realise something done silently is more pleasing and satisfying.

They have all the abilities as any living or dead legend but they are the people who are in the background, the champion makers. We know thousands of living legends at present. People appreciate what they do but we do not realise, there is always someone in the background who is the backbone of others' success. We never bothered to know because we are so busy admiring the current champions.

All the Olympic medal winners have coaches; their achievements would be minor if they did not receive coaching. At the same time, all these coaches have setbacks too. Maybe when they were young, they had the ability but missed their mark due to a lack of coaching or facilities. Now they want to make sure you, as their student, can achieve what they could not. This way they feel satisfied too.

Many saints have their gurus who have shown the path towards enlightenment. You would have been nothing without their spark but they remain anonymous. We know the names of the first three people who landed on the moon in 1969; we never know how many people worked in the background to accomplish their mission. We know the legends but the makers of legends are always unknown.

I call them silent legends and I felt like writing a few words to show our appreciation. I am a simple man; there was the effort of so many spiritual people to make me who I am and provide me with what I know. Without their help, I would not know as much or be as successful. Above all, God, Satnam Ji and Paul Ji made sure that I was spiritually trained. **God is behind every legend ever created,**

But it is Silent.

SHER GILL Galib

London

SPIRITUAL TERMINOLOGY

Akashic Records: The total record of our physical incarnations which are kept in the causal plane. On that basis; Past, present and future can be predicted.

Angels of Death: Assistants of the king of dead to collect the departing soul from physical at their last hour.

Astral Body: Radiant or emotional body. Astral plane; next plane above physical.

Astrology: It is the study of planets and their position concerning your date of birth, the future can be predicted.

Aura: Is a magnetic field that surrounds all souls to express its spiritual status.

Brahma: The lord of mental plane and one of the Hindu trinity Gods. Brahma, Vishnu and Shiva.

Buddhi: Intellectual: Is part of the mind, the chief instrument of thought.

Cause & Effect: Action and reaction lead to creating negative or positive karma.

Chakra(s): Psychic centres in the human body; all yoga practitioners use these centres to have spiritual experience.

Conscience: Is moral or ethical development in person.

Consciousness: That state of being in which the individual lives all-day

Creation: Whatever has been created by God for training purposes.

Creed (God's): All life flows from God itself; nothing can exist without spirit or the will of God.

Crown Chakra: The soft spot at the top in the human skull and easy passage for soul travel into the spiritual planes.

Cult: Is a system of worship of Master, deity, Ideal or any celebrity.

Deja vu: Is the ability to know the events before happening.

Direct projection: It is the technique to move soul and body together instantly.

Dreams: It is a way of Spirit to communicate with all souls. The spiritual Master also communicate with Seekers, known as dream teachings.

Enlightenment: The state of spiritual knowledge and awakening within.

Eternity: Expression of life without a sense of time and space, the present spiritual dwelling is always in eternity.

Etheric plane: The unconscious plane or dividing line between the mental and soul plane. Sub-conscious mind.

Faith: Is the keystone to have any spiritual success. It is the belief in Master or teachings to achieve the set goal.

Free will: God's gift to each soul to decide how to create karma or live life.

Haiome: One of the most powerful spiritual **words**, it can lead the Seeker to God.

Hypnotism: One of the psychic arts to balance many disorders or to practice evil.

Imagination: It is a mental faculty to activate positive vibrations to have an inner experience or soul travel.

Immortality: It is a state of being, deathless or as opposed to mortality.

Incarnations: The continuous cycle of births and deaths in the physical world.

Individuality: The Immortal self of each soul has its own identity; no two souls are the same as twins.

Jot-Niranjan: The ruler on astral plane and powerhouse to the physical world.

Kal: Is the overall in-charge of negative Spirit.

Karma: The law of cause & effect. It is the decisive part of human suffering.

King of the Dead: Is the lord of karma on the astral plane that judges the souls' journey according to its earned karma.

Light & Sound: Are twin pillars of God or is Spirit.

Love: It is the love force of God that sustains all creation and balance of all universes. There is human love and impersonal love.

Magic: It is trickery or part of illusion to please the audience.

Manifestation: Manifested, which is normally apparent to the physical senses.

Meditation: Is the practice of sitting while reciting spiritual **word** for esoteric experience.

Mental plane: Is the fourth plane in God's world. The sound is of 'running water'.

Mind: The thinking part of human consciousness or the chief instrument for soul's survival in the lower worlds.

Ocean of love and Mercy: Life-giving spirit. Love, for the wellbeing of all creation.

Omnipotence: All-powerful. omnipresence; present. omniscience; all-knowing.

Par-Brahm: He is the lord on etheric plane.

Para-Vidya: Is spiritual knowledge. **Apara**-vidya; is physical knowledge.

Philosophy: It is psychic or core study of the religions by use of the mental faculties.

Physical plane: Is the lowest plane of matter, energy, space and time.

Power: There is supreme or neuter power and negative & positive operates in the lower worlds. Political or any other authority in this world is also power.

Prayers: Is an approach to contacting a spiritual Master or God. It could be a request or to feel its presence. If you know God is within, it will understand your needs.

Prophecy: Spiritual man who can forecast future events long before they happen.

Psychic Space: It is the natural right of each soul to feel free. Be yourself and let the others be.

Re-incarnation: It is the circle of each soul, birth- death and rebirth.

Religions: Are spiritual and social systems created in the name of a religious guru.

Sach Khand: Is in the fifth plane of God world. It is the first pure spirit plane and the ruler is Satnam.

Sahasara-Dal-Kanwal: The capital city of astral plane and meeting place between the Master and Seeker after sun & moon worlds.

Satnam Ji: The first personification of God to be seen in male form. Humans are created, replicas of Satnam Ji. Lord of soul plane. The sound is of a single-note flute.

Satya-Yuga: Golden age: This yuga lasted for 1,728,000 years.

Seeker: Disciple: Who has the yearning within to experience God in this lifetime.

Self-realisation: Knowledge of its existence as soul and have answers to self, such as; Who am I? Where am I going after death and how to reach there?

Self-Surrender: Complete submission to the Master and principles of teachings you follow.

Soul: Atma: Is a unit of God-awareness. It is a micro part of the macro.

Soul Travel: Is the change in the state of consciousness or the means of travelling to other planes.

Space and Time: Space means nothing apart from our perception of objects and time means nothing apart from our experience of events.

Spirit: It is the combined of light and sound. It is the adhesive or life force of all universes.

Spiritual Freedom: Is liberation from the lower worlds or the wheel of eighty-four.

Spiritual unfoldment: Is to become aware of what God has invested within us.

Spirituality: Is the essence of spiritual experience, which cannot be taught but can be caught.

Sub-conscious mind: The unconscious or the reactive mind.

Sufism: Is Islamic mysticism and total dedication to Allah.

Total awareness: It is the ultimate goal for all spiritual Seekers to achieve on this path.

Trinity of God: God, Spirit and the Master. Father, Son and Holy ghost.

Truth: Is the only source of knowledge and man is the mirror of truth. You cannot receive more than what your soul can hold.

Vibrations: Spiritual waves we carry as our aura will show on our countenance.

Will of God: Is God's ultimate decision and nothing can exist without this will of God.

Will power: Indicates the maturity in each person. The strength of execution.

Wisdom: Is spiritual knowledge beyond all intellectual ability.

Word of God: Shabda, spirit or the flow of spirit from God.

Lightning Source UK Ltd.
Milton Keynes UK
UKHW012056020123
414736UK00002B/26

9 781803 811864